THE
STEPCHILDREN

STEPHANIE SPARKS

For my family

THE
STEPCHILDREN

BEFORE

"**C**all me Daddy," he said.

Fifteen-year-old Jamie Riley choked down the bland lump of cold, leftover wedding cake as she stared up at her stepfather, towering over her in his tan slacks and itchy sweater vest. It sure beat the obnoxiously white tuxedo he wore the day before. His muddy brown eyes bulged, magnified behind his thick-lensed glasses. Clutching a glass of warm milk, he rubbed at the milk mustache coating the bristles under his nose, not quite swiping it away.

The guy was a dork. From the day her mother sprang him on her — "Jamie, honey? I want you to meet some-one" — to the moment he donned his wedding day best, Jamie rolled her eyes at his royal dorkiness.

At first, she paid him no mind, because he was just

another guy in her mother's long list of losers, following in her father's footsteps. She figured he wouldn't last.

Burt was not like the others. He proposed to Christine after three months of dating, though Jamie suspected they had kept their coupling a secret for a few months before telling her. They tittered like teenagers when Christine gave him a tour of the house — *their house. Not his.*

He strutted around the place, eyeballing their family photos and critiquing Jamie's drawings, like he was some high-brow art critic. He straightened the frames on the wall and wiped dust away with his index finger. He prowled about, taking everything in. Looming over the mother and daughter in the living room, he was too tall for their house. Simply, he wasn't a good fit.

"I'm not calling him anything," Jamie vowed the night before the wedding. She toyed with her mother's veil. The wedding itself was lavish and unnecessary, but Christine never got a dream wedding with Jamie's dad. They married in a friend's backyard a month before Jamie was born.

"You don't have to call him anything," Christine conceded. "Just Burt. And if one day you want to call him 'Dad,' that's okay too."

Jamie had a dad already. Just not a very involved one. Tanner Riley was a deadbeat husband who walked out on them when Jamie was only eight. He came back from time to time to pay up his child support and take Jamie for soft-serve ice cream down the street. But he never had any fatherly wisdom to impart or love to give. He was more like a fun uncle, grinding up all his money and energy into getting his band off the ground.

When Tanner walked out on them, Christine uprooted

her daughter. She convinced her parents to help her buy a house in the Port Coquitlam neighborhood of Mary Hill with its rolling hills, established trees, and unique 70s-era homes.

They lived seven happy years there before Burt wiped his loafers on their welcome mat. The house became his almost overnight.

Jamie set aside the piece of cake, swiped from the fridge. A late-night snack for a late-night study session. Her mother may have just gotten married, but that didn't make her mountain of homework go away.

"Uh, what?" she asked as Burt reached across her desk and snatched the fork from her hand. "Hey!"

He forked himself a big bite, cramming the dessert into his mouth. Crumbs spewed out, littering her textbooks. Then he gulped down his milk, wiping his mouth with his thumb and forefinger, pinky and ring finger curled around the fork. His gold wedding band flashed. All the while, a whiny wind whistled through his nose.

"Mmm, that's good!" Then he added, "I just stopped in to say goodnight."

She rolled her eyes. "Goodnight, Burt."

"We're family now," he said. "Call me Daddy."

"Don't think so," she mumbled. Scowling, she reached for her sketchpad, hidden under her bio notes, and began scribbling. She hoped he would get the hint and go away.

"It's a little late for that, Jelly Bean," he said, pushing his nickname on her.

"Don't call me that."

Her desk lamp cruelly cast his long shadow against her door, making him even more imposing. "Time for lights out."

Ugh. Eye roll. "It's *only* eleven. And Mom lets me stay up as late as I want."

"Well, your mother and I had a discussion about that, and we think you would do better in school if you got the proper amount of sleep. A solid eight hours always does wonders for me."

"I'm trying to do my homework."

"It looks like you're doodling."

She shot him a frosty look. "It's for art class."

"Oh, really?" He raised an eyebrow over his dated frames, snatching the book out from under her. Her pencil scratched the paper, leaving a dark, unwanted, and impossible-to-erase mark. Her picture was ruined. Burt frowned, turning it from side to side. "I can't even tell what this is." He knocked on her bio textbook. "I'd recommend hitting these books. Art is not your ... strong point."

His opinion didn't hold water with her. Not only was he a dork, but he was a boring, old real estate agent who liked bugs. He didn't have an artistic bone in his body and he wouldn't know good art if it walked up and bit his nose.

Yet, the criticism stung.

"Give it back," she demanded.

He tucked the pad under his arm. "It's time for bed."

"Give it *back.*"

Shadows grew longer, deeper on his face. The reflection on his lenses masked his dark eyes. *"I won't tell you again."*

Grumbling, she jumped up from her desk and slammed the chair against it, which rattled the mirror against the wall and shook the lamp. She stormed to her bed, pulled back the comforter, and plopped down, arms crossed.

"There. Happy now?"

He pointed to the lamp. "You forgot to turn out the light."

She puckered her face. "I want it on."

"I said it was time for lights out. Turn. Off. The. Light."

"Back off," she muttered. She knew how the words sounded coming out of her mumbling mouth, but she would never actually swear at an adult. Her mother would lose her shit. But Burt didn't know her well enough, just as she didn't know anything about him. Yet.

But he didn't yell or run off to tell her mother. He took two swift steps to her desk, wrapped his fist around her lamp, and pulled. The cord stretched, knocking her papers and books to the floor. He gave it one good, hard yank. Darkness blanketed the room.

Unsettled, she couldn't see where he had gone — until his breath hit her cheek. "Don't you ever *fuck* with me," he snarled. "And from now on, you call me Daddy. We're family now, so you better start acting like it."

He dropped the sketchpad on her thighs with a slap.

Then he left, the lamp cord trailing behind him.

She clutched the pad to her chest. *Fucking psycho,* she thought, tears threatening to spill.

She didn't know the half of it.

CHAPTER 1

13 years later...
October, Tuesday night

Jamie stormed into the session simmering with rage — at her mom, at her landlord. Hell, even at Dr. Henshaw and the others for cutting into her Tuesday evenings every single week for the past several months. And for what? Bland coffee and reliving past trauma?

She was also mad at herself — pushing thirty with nothing to show for it.

But as she sat in a squeaky folding chair, waiting for a turn to speak, her irritation subsided. For that, she blamed the chill atmosphere, the dim lighting, the patter of rain hitting the window. And Kay.

Karolyn Quigley ("Kay to my friends!") was such a beautiful, kind, bubbly person inside and out, it almost made Jamie sick. She probably would have hated Kay for no good reason if she didn't also feel guilty that she was stuck in a wheelchair — guilty because she should have stopped Burt before he put her there.

Kay never got too worked up in the meetings, or pissed off and ranting like Benji Martin, or sullen and quiet like Jamie. She sat quietly and dabbed at her eyes with a crumpled tissue and relived the trauma they all knew too well — because everyone in that circle, save for Henshaw, had at one time been the stepchild of Burt Mengle, the Family Man Killer.

Kay talked about hearing "Sweet Caroline" as one of her triggers. Back when Burt was her stepdad, he would wander through the house whistling it, or he would sneak up on her to belt it out suddenly. "It's not even my *name,*" she said. "But you know Burt. He thinks he's so clever."

They all knew Burt.

"He used to sing *Benji* and the Jets," grumbled Benji, his shoulders hunched. His long arms dangled between his legs to fiddle with his coffee cup, which he had placed on the floor. "I fucking hate that song."

Jamie looked around the circle. Across from her, Henshaw sat, holding a yellow legal pad on her lap. She never wrote anything down, just listened and tapped the end of her pencil against her lips, gazing at them from behind her thick-lensed glasses and long, salt-and-pepper bangs. Each week, she wore a different frumpy sweater that matched the neutral carpet and decor of her small office.

Between Henshaw and Jamie sat Kay. Benji slouched in his seat on Jamie's right, and if he wasn't fidgeting, his knee bounced up and down like a jackhammer. Jamie wanted to stab a pen through his kneecap some sessions, but reminded herself that she wasn't a violent person.

Except for that one time thirteen years ago.

Her chest tightened and she sat up straighter. Her turn to share was next. She tried too hard to focus on Kay's update — *what are you doing to improve your mindset this week?* — but her attention drifted to the empty seat next to Henshaw. She wondered what his excuse would be this time.

"Jamie?" interrupted Henshaw. "Would you like to tell us about your week?"

She averted her eyes to the handbag between her sneakers. The edge of an envelope jutted out. The sight of the plain, brown paper got her hackles up, but she couldn't imagine herself following Kay's story with one about her passive-aggressive landlord and her petty phone tag fights with her runaway mom.

"Uh, no, pretty boring."

Her response had been anything but when she opened her mail to find the letter.

Dear Ms. Riley — It has come to our attention that you are operating a home business out of your rental unit... As such we are giving you 30 days' notice before increasing your monthly rental payments...

Thirty days! On top of that, the increase was substantial, enough to ensure she would have to cut back on her bills or try to get a break on her student loan payments, or sell all her furniture online just to cover the next three months.

Plus, the letter was cowardly. She saw her landlord every week. They were friendly. Jamie would always help bring other people's packages into the secure part of the building whenever the delivery guy couldn't be bothered.

Why didn't he just mention it in the hallway?

When she called to bitch him out, he very calmly explained that the rent increase was necessary. Costs were going up and it was very expensive for him to run the building. But Jamie was a dog with a bone, yapping after him about what a dick move it was.

Finally, her landlord pulled out the big guns. *It's against the bylaws to operate a business out of your unit.*

"But I don't— I mean, it's just graphic design stuff. It's not like I have clients over—" *to see the shitty hovel I live in.* She omitted that part and instead went with her old standby, *"It's not fair!"* Not surprisingly the tactic she took with her mother didn't convince the landlord.

She needed money fast. Moving was not an option — it was too expensive to find a place on such short notice. She had no savings and her freelance gigs had dried up. So she did something radical and called her mom.

After three rings, her call went to voicemail. "Mom, my landlord is being a dick. I need money. Can you send me an e-transfer?"

Henshaw tapped her pencil on her notepad. "Pretty boring, you say?"

Jamie nodded, feeling like a little kid ashamed of her greedy behavior. She didn't want to talk about it — not when the others were having real problems, like Kay's workplace not accommodating her wheelchair.

"No complaints," she said, molars grinding.

Henshaw checked her watch. "Okay, then I—"

Benji put his hand up. His complexion was so pink and youthful and ruddy that he looked like a plastic doll smothered in freckles. "I just wanna say I tried using the showers at the gym the other day."

Henshaw nodded. It was her only tell that she was impressed or happy. "What prompted that decision, Benji?"

"I don't know. I was really fuckin' sweaty, I guess? And it seemed way grosser to bring all those germs into my truck for the drive home, ya know?"

Jamie sat up, paying attention. Though she did not want to imagine Benji in the shower, it was a big deal that he used a public one.

Benji had developed a fear of germs and garbage as a child, when he was forced to hide in a Dumpster the night Burt murdered his family. The slime soaked through his pajamas, and the wretched, rotting stench of fruit suffocated him — meanwhile, all he could do was listen to his brothers crying and his mother screaming.

The police found him hours later, sucking his thumb and stinking of trash.

But Jamie had listened to his story before, had heard his rants about the grime collecting in public showers — second in grossness to bathtubs, which he described as putrid cesspools of bacteria.

As Jamie buckled in to hear it all over again, the door opened and *he* walked in.

Nick Michaels.

Jamie's heart skipped a beat at the sight of him.

He had his jean jacket collar popped up to protect his neck and ears from the cold autumn air. His blue eyes squinted, adjusting to the dim light in the group space. Dripping wet, he swept his thick, dark hair back from his forehead. A raindrop hung off a missed strand, and Jamie ached to reach out and collect it on her fingertip as proof that the beautiful, broken boy had returned.

Except Nick wasn't a boy — he was a twenty-five-year-old man.

He shook the rain off his jacket, before peeling the wet denim off his skin and hanging it over the back of an empty chair. A tight, black t-shirt stretched across his broad chest and thick biceps. Crossing his arms, he took a seat and slouched down with his long legs pointing into the circle.

"Thanks for joining us, Nick," welcomed Henshaw.

"Sorry I'm late," he muttered.

"That's alright. We're just glad you could make it for this part."

"This part?" asked Kay. "Are we doing something different?"

"Not exactly," she said. "I have some news to share, and I thought it would be best if we all heard it together. We're stronger as a group, remember?"

"Yeah, sure," sneered Benji. "So what's the big news?"

Henshaw paused, letting the group collect themselves. Kay tipped her head to the side and Benji cracked his knuckles. Nick gazed at his motorcycle boots, lost in his own thoughts. But Jamie tensed. Fingers laced together, she pressed one thumb against the other until the nail turned white.

"Before it gets out in the news," Henshaw continued, "I thought you should know… Burt Mengle is dead."

CHAPTER 2

Burt Valentine. Hubert Simmons. Bernie Smits. Burt
Fisher. The man had a lot of aliases. One for every
family. Which made sense. He couldn't be a
notorious, family-slaughtering fugitive and go about his
life in Vancouver's Lower Mainland while continuing to
sign marriage certificates using his actual name.

When he went by Mengle, Burt had the perfect job. He
taught junior high science and would proudly bring in his
collection of preserved butterflies to show off to his
students. The kids would stick out their tongues and cry,
"Yuck!" to which Burt would eagerly defend his
collection. He joked that he loved them more than his own
family. In hindsight, it wasn't a joke — because Burt
never joked.

On the surface, he had the perfect family. Two boys
and a girl, a loving wife. A modest house in a nice,
suburban neighborhood. He drove an economical car and

threw summer BBQs for his neighbors and coworkers. It was exactly the kind of picture-perfect family life that made for the juicy beginning of a true crime mystery.

The children's sweet faces covered paperbacks and the Mengles' private lives became fodder for armchair detectives and podcast hosts — *what made "bad dad" Burt Mengle snap?*

Snap. Jamie hated that word. It implied the one who snapped had no control over their actions. Burt planned every minute detail of his crimes. He just never accounted for the resiliency and cunning of his stepchildren.

After murdering his entire family, he disappeared. People suspected he went into hiding in the Rocky Mountains, or that he continued his reign of terror along the Highway of Tears. No one guessed that he simply laid low: changed his name, waited until the heat died down, and latched on to a new unsuspecting family.

And no one imagined he would do this several times.

He left few survivors in his wake, but the children that survived grew up. Messed up and broken — physically and mentally — they were brought together after the trial by Dr. Henshaw, who wanted to form a support group for troubled childhood trauma victims. "Survivors of Burt" or "Burt's Kids," they quipped at their first meeting.

"Do we really have to name this?" said Nick, scraping the toe of his boot on the carpet. It had only been their first session and he already had one foot out the door.

"No," agreed Jamie, but in her mind, it was clear what their name was, what united them. They were *the Stepchildren.*

* * *

After several long moments of silence while the group processed Henshaw's words, Kay burst into tears. She covered her face and sobbed. Jamie thought about reaching over to pat her back, but her own disturbed memories of Burt kept her frozen in place.

She touched the back of her head, feeling her way down her short, bobbed haircut until she could rub her neck. She hadn't worn her hair long since Burt ripped a chunk out of her scalp. She remembered as she fell, seeing him slumped against the wall where the staircase turned, his grip pulsing around the clump of her hair.

"Jesus fuck!" snapped Benji, smacking his hand against his thigh.

He startled Jamie. She blinked as if waking up from a nightmare — only to wake into another nightmare.

"What are you feeling right now, Benji?" asked Henshaw.

Benji paused. No one dared to interrupt him in case he went off again, like a red-headed powder keg. He wiped his nose. His knees bounced up and down, faster than before. "Fuckin'... Fuckin' *good* — that's what I feel!"

Henshaw tapped her pencil. "Care to explain?"

He leaned back, taking in the others. He pointed at Jamie. "I don't get your sour face or why Kay's crying. This is fucking good news. The son of a bitch is dead. I hope he got fuckin' shivved, or—"

"Benji!" squeaked Kay.

"Hey, I'm just saying what we're all thinking."

Nick sighed, reaching around for his jacket. "Was that everything?"

"Well, yes," said Henshaw. "But I thought we might take some time to talk about this. Kay, do you have anything to add?"

Shaking her head, Kay wiped her tears and put on a brave smile. "I don't know what to say… Just that… *it's over.* It's finally over!"

"I can drink to that," said Benji, hoisting his coffee cup to his mouth.

"How about you, Nick?"

He shrugged. "Nah."

Jamie sneaked a glance at him. He was achingly handsome with his dark blue eyes, sharp cheekbones, pouty lips — and that long, loose strand of hair. It dangled over his scarred eyebrow.

Though he never mentioned it, Jamie knew who gave him that scar.

But when Nick did talk, mumbling his answers to Henshaw's questions, he would run his hand through his hair, brushing it out of his eyes. Then the second he stopped speaking, his head would tilt down and the hair would fall back over his face, hiding him and his emotions from the others.

Jamie badly wanted to help him heal.

I can't even fix my own problems.

She sighed into her knuckles, daydreaming about saving him, when Henshaw caught her attention. She smiled kindly, waving her notepad. "Jamie? Are you still with us?"

How long was I thinking about…? She glanced at Nick. He stared back at her, his attention making her skin heat up. She quickly looked away.

"Uh, yeah. How did he…?"

Henshaw lowered her notepad. "An autopsy hasn't yet been done, but I was told he passed away in his sleep."

"Lucky fuck," grumbled Benji.

"In his cell?"

Henshaw's brow furrowed. "Yes, why? What are you feeling?"

It wasn't just Nick that she wanted to fix. It was Benji and Kay too. Children of all the families Burt destroyed—even his own. He had cut such a wide swath of destruction that healing seemed impossible for anyone who had crossed his path.

What happened to Nick, Benji, and Kay's families was all Jamie's fault. She didn't share Burt's killer instinct. Her stomach churned when she thought back to the moment she drove a screwdriver into his knee. If only she had killed him when she had the chance, none of them would be in that room. They would all be living normal lives. Kay would get to run marathons, and Benji wouldn't be so goddamn angry all the time, and maybe Nick would crack a smile. She bet he had an amazing one.

As for Jamie… If she had to go through therapy for the rest of her life to deal with killing a man, then she would do it.

But that's not how real life played out. She let Burt get away. She ran to her mother for comfort when she should have made sure he was dead, and he escaped.

She couldn't let that happen again.

"Jamie?" Henshaw pressed. "Do you want to share your thoughts with the group?"

Jamie cleared her throat and rubbed her face where tears would be if quaked with bone-shaking anger or nerve-rattling anxiety.

Instead, she felt strangely calm.

"He's not dead."

CHAPTER 3

Jamie's words stopped time. No one spoke, no one moved. Except for Dr. Henshaw, who scrambled to make notes on her legal pad. In her frenzy, the tip of her pencil snapped. Scrunching up her face, she brushed it aside and concentrated on her patient.

"Can you elaborate?" she asked.

An embarrassed heat crept up Jamie's neck yet again, and she focused on the floor. "Umm, well, you know…"

He's not dead.

Benji's brows raised, wrinkling up his forehead. "You think he's still *alive?*"

"Well, just not dead."

"What does that mean?"

"He's not dead," she repeated.

Benji slapped his thighs. "Does anyone know what the hell she's talking about?"

"I understand this news may be challenging for you,"

said Henshaw.

"It's not," said Jamie, wiping her palms on her jeans. She nervously dared to look around the group, avoiding Nick at the last second. "You guys can't seriously believe he's for real? After all the times he faked his death or just disappeared?"

"I confirmed it myself," said Henshaw.

Kay's head tipped to one side. "What don't you believe, Jamie?"

"Did you see the body?" she asked Henshaw.

Nick and Benji groaned and Kay froze. Henshaw reminded everyone that if they weren't comfortable with Jamie's remarks then they could change the subject.

Nick crossed his arms. "It's fine."

"Did you see him?" Jamie pressed.

Henshaw slowly shook her head. "No, Jamie, I didn't. I spoke to an administrator at the prison."

Jamie was about to say something else, but everyone was staring at her. Each face reflected a combination of disgust, fear, and impatience. She looked back down. "Never mind."

"Why do you think he's still alive?" asked Henshaw.

Benji sighed again, shaking his head

Kay covered her mouth, rubbing her lips.

Nick stayed seated, his body tensed and eager to bolt. They wanted to hear Jamie's answer. Her fears were theirs too.

She crossed her arms and puffed up her chest. When she spoke, she forced herself to look at the others. "He doesn't die. He makes you *think* he's dead and then he finds another family to suck the life out of. We'd all be pretty fucking stupid if we thought for a second that he's *actually* dead." Her face burned even hotter. Anxious sweat made her armpits itch. Then she added quietly, "I think we need to see for ourselves."

"See what?" asked Kay.

Benji groaned again. "No way. That's fuckin' gross."

"What?" Kay was lost.

"She wants to see the body."

"Burt's body?" Kay's eyes bugged out of her head as turned to Jamie. "Are you serious? What difference would it make?"

Praying that the floor would crack apart and swallow her whole, Jamie said nothing. *I shouldn't have said anything. I should have kept it to myself.*

"If you need to be certain, I can look into getting a copy of the death certificate," offered Henshaw. "But there's no reason for any of you to see the body, and actually, doing so could add to the trauma you're already dealing with."

Jamie avoided Henshaw's sympathetic gaze. *Too late for that.*

* * *

As soon as the session ended, Jamie leaped out of her seat. Embarrassment drove every step. She would have been the first to leave had Nick not been closer to the exit. He threw the door open. Jamie caught it with her elbow. She grunted, which got Nick's attention.

He threw a look over his shoulder. "Sorry," he said. "Didn't see you."

She shrugged, reaching for her phone, hoping to get lost in the dark depths of her bag. There was still no reply from her mom about her rent problem, but at least the phone could help her avoid an awkward conversation with Nick, since his mere presence tied her tongue.

He turned back to her from the stairwell exit, holding the door this time. "You taking the stairs?"

"Uh…" No one else was waiting for the elevator yet, which meant it would take a minute or two for the damn thing to arrive, and by then, Benji and Kay would be there, and Nick would be long gone. "Yeah, trying to get more steps in," she said, following him down with a shaky smile.

Nick moved fast, already rounding the next flight of stairs. She was relieved to be rid of him.

He slowed on the next turn, letting her catch up before resuming his pace. "You really think he might still be alive?"

"Um…" She had hoped not to have to answer any follow-up questions to her outburst. "I just want to be sure, you know? Don't you?"

"I don't know. I try not to think about him."

They made it to the main floor lobby, a glassed-in space with a sign pointing to all the various specialists' offices: a dentist, a physiotherapist, Henshaw's practice, and a registry office. It was after hours for all the others, so the lobby was dimly lit to save energy.

The elevator dinged, hatching open to release Benji and Kay. Nick nodded at them, holding the main door for the whole crew.

"Can't believe you wanna go see a dead body," said Benji, shaking his head.

"It's finally over," said Kay. "Why not leave it alone?"

Jamie gnashed her molars together. "You *know* why."

As she stepped out into the cool fall air in the nearly empty parking lot, she kept an eye on her faded maroon RAV4, parked under an orange-yellow lot light. She parked under that light every session to ensure no one lurked around her car when she exited the building.

"Ding dong, the dick is dead!" hollered Benji, as he swung off a pole. "If anything, we should all go celebrate with some beers down at Darby's. I'll get the first round."

"I gotta run," said Nick, clapping Benji on the back. "You guys have one for me, though."

With a grin, Benji turned to Jamie and Kay. "How about it, ladies? Two girls, one cup?"

"Gross," said Jamie.

"Yeah, Benji, gross." Kay pointed to an idling van parked on the street. "I can't anyway. My aunt's waiting."

"Bring her along," he said. "I like older chicks."

Kay shot him a stern, but playful look as she wheeled toward it. "See you guys next week." She waved at Nick, giving him a soft smile. "Bye, Nick!"

Benji walked alongside Jamie until she was at her RAV and he was at his big, black pickup truck. "Man, we get the best news of our fucking lives and no one wants to celebrate? Fuckin' weak, man."

"Sorry," she said, struggling to get her key in the lock.

"Hey, maybe next week then? You know, when the doc proves he's actually bit the bullet?"

"Sure, Benj." But Jamie doubted Henshaw's proof would be enough to convince her. She needed to see for herself.

CHAPTER 4

Overnight, the idea of seeing Burt's corpse implanted itself in Jamie's brain, and like a parasite, it began systematically shutting down all logical thoughts. All Jamie could do was follow through.

"Hello, my name is Jamie Mengle." The words tasted sour in her mouth. "I'm calling to find out where my stepfather's body has been taken. My mother's unable to handle the funeral arrangements right now, as you can probably imagine, so I said I would take care of it. Would you happen to know if…?"

It was almost too easy. The administrator at the prison was sympathetic and only too helpful to give Jamie just enough information to figure out that the body had been moved to a funeral home in Chilliwack.

From there, she jumped on Google and found three funeral homes in the area. Then she began calling.

She hated talking on the phone; most of her communications with clients began and ended with email. She hated the whine in her voice and the way it croaked when she first said hello, like her vocal cords had rusted from a lack of a social life. But in this case, not calling wasn't an option.

The Bartleby Funeral Home answered after a few rings, and Jamie again explained that she was the stepdaughter of Burt Mengle and she was overseeing the funeral arrangements. The funeral director seemed a little flustered, but answered her questions.

"All of the arrangements are taken care of," said Mr. Bartleby. "There will be no service and he will be interred on Saturday."

It was almost noon on Wednesday. She had less than three days to see the body.

"Thank you," she said.

After she hung up, a notification popped up that she had four weeks until her rent increased. She hit ignore, thinking there were more important things she had to deal with, but what was more important than keeping a roof over her head? Burt was dead — calling the funeral home con-firmed it. His corpse was on a slab getting pumped full of embalming fluid.

She needed to call her mom, not drive to a Chilliwack funeral home and— *And then what?*

She hadn't hit any roadblocks yet. No signs that she should turn back now. Might as well see the mission through to the end.

But first she needed to resolve her money problems.

Summoning her courage, she dialed her mom. "Hey, it's me," she said, after the call went to voicemail. Again.

"Where are you? Have you been getting my messages? I need something. Call me back."

Her phone vibrated. Her eyes blurred, and for a moment she saw her mom's name appear on screen. *CHRISTINE RILEY*. She blinked. Disappointment sank in. She had misread it.

KAROLYN QUIGLEY.

Except for one time to pass along the word that a session had been canceled because Dr. Henshaw had the flu, Kay never called. Nor did Benji or Nick. They weren't friends. Just four acquaintances with a shared trauma. But when they started group therapy together, they figured it would be helpful to stay connected and reach out to talk.

None of them ever did.

"Hi, Jamie. It's Kay. Are you busy?"

Jamie looked down at her to-do list, which earlier in the summer had been a list of logos and product design pieces she needed to complete. Today all she had written down were the phone numbers of the prison and a few funeral homes. She scribbled out the numbers.

"Not especially. What's up?"

"Okay, well, remember what we were talking about last night?"

"Mm-hm." She began to sketch a tombstone with Burt's name on it as Kay talked.

"I was thinking about what you said…"

"Oh, yeah. Sorry if I upset you. Sometimes it seems like Benji sucks all the air out of the room and I forget myself."

"You're right."

"About Benji?"

"No." Kay lowered her voice to a whisper. Jamie

imagined her looking around conspiratorially, making sure her nosy aunt wasn't eavesdropping. *"About Burt."*

"You believe me?"

"I don't know," Kay admitted. "I used to believe that I was a princess and someday a prince would come and sweep me off my feet. But now my feet are dead to me and there aren't many princes to go around."

"Okay…"

"And I was Burt's stepkid once too, so I think you're right."

"You think he's still alive."

"Not necessarily. But I think you're right that we need to make sure. It's our responsibility to…" She choked up.

Palms sweating, Jamie pressed the phone against her ear as if she could push through to Kay's side and hear every last word. She held her breath, not daring to speak. Afraid to startle her.

Kay sniffled, starting over. "I just think it's our responsibility to make sure that creep doesn't do this to anyone ever again."

Jamie couldn't agree more, though having someone on her side for once was an unfamiliar feeling. "Thanks."

"You're welcome. So now what?"

"I'm going to see the body."

"You know where it is?"

"Yeah."

"Then I'm coming with you."

"You don't have to do that."

But Kay's mind was set. When she decided on something, it was next to impossible to change her mind. "Do we have to go to the prison? If so, I'm going to need a ride. I don't think my aunt would want me to go anywhere near that place."

"You don't have to," Jamie replied. "I know where he is."

"Good. When do we go?"

* * *

That night, the four stepchildren met at Darby's pub. Jamie hadn't planned for a field trip. Having four people go to a funeral home to see a body was unusual. If they would only let her go on her own, she could go during the day and try to talk her way in. But Jamie admittedly wasn't particularly charming or sincere, and they knew she wouldn't get far.

Besides, Kay was adamant about this mission being a team effort.

"We need to do this because we're stronger together. We'll finally have closure."

Jamie didn't care what the others needed for closure. And she was a bit miffed that they had decided to take over her plans when just the other night, they had written her off as a sicko. But when Kay said she was scared about Burt faking them out, the two young men rushed to her aid. Beautiful, soft-spoken Kay had a way with men. She batted her big, Bambi eyelashes and they fell at her feet. Nick and Benji were suckers for it. So if Kay impressed upon them the need to see the body together, they wouldn't question *her*.

They gathered at a table near the back of the pub. Jamie arrived after Kay. Benji followed, making small talk as they waited for Nick, who arrived last but on time, swinging his keychain around his finger.

"Whose car are we taking?" he asked, getting right down to business.

"I got the pickup," said Benji, "but I got too much work shit in the backseat. Won't fit all of us."

"Well, I brought the Mustang," said Nick, who seemed to have a new car every time Jamie saw him, thanks to his body shop business. "But sorry, Kay — it won't fit your chair."

"Don't be sorry," she said, touching his arm. "I don't even have a car! And Chilliwack's a long drive."

Jamie sighed. "I guess it's up to me."

"Well, it was your plan to begin with," Benji pointed out.

I don't have a plan, she thought, leading them out into the rain.

But she did. Once she proved to them that he was still alive, her plan was to make sure Burt Mengle was dead once and for all.

CHAPTER 5

The rain lightened as Jamie turned off the Trans Canada Highway and into Chilliwack. She was too focused on making the correct turn to flick off the wiper blades, squeaking across the windshield, that Benji startled her when he reached between the front seats and did it for her.

"Hey!"

"Hey, what?" he shot back. "That sound was makin' me nuts."

She pointed at the tiny drops hitting the glass. "It's still raining."

"So? Let it accumulate."

Jamie scowled at him in the rearview mirror. "Wow, that's a big word for you."

"What're you sayin'? That I'm dumb or something?"

"Or something."

"Knock it off," said Nick. He didn't raise his voice, but his tone got their attention.

Jamie gulped, worried that he thought even less of her than he did already. If she was quick to bicker over windshield wipers, she was probably no better than Benji.

"Are we there yet?" asked Kay, vying for the title of Most Annoying Person of the Roadtrip.

"Soon," Jamie said. "Let me see…"

It was dark out. Rain clouds smothered out any light from the night sky, and the street she had turned down had few functioning streetlights. The road was black, the sky was black, and everything in between was gray and blurred. She tried to breathe through the oppressive feeling that the universe was caving in on her.

Nick's hand shot out between the seats. His arm rubbed against her shoulder, as he pointed to a sign she blew past.

"That way," he said.

She slammed on the breaks. Everyone flew forward. Kay gasped, bracing against the dashboard. The wheel-chair rattled and banged around in the back. Benji swore. Nick gripped Jamie's headrest, as she frantically spun the wheel.

The RAV hydroplaned across the road. Cars honked behind them.

Jamie managed to turn, quietly letting out a shaky breath, and before long, they pulled into the empty parking lot of the Bartleby Funeral Home.

"Shit," muttered Benji, wiping his face. "Next time, I'm gonna drive."

"There won't be a next time," Kay said softly.

"Jesus Christ," he grumbled, throwing open the door.

"That's ominous as fuck."

"I didn't mean to be," she said. "I just really want him to be dead."

Don't we all.

"Where are you going?" asked Nick, as Benji jumped out.

"Getting some fresh goddamn air," he replied. "What does it look like?"

"It looks like we oughta park at the back." Nick pointed a thumb at the blacked-out building. The only light on was a glowing neon sign that said CLOSED.

"Why?" asked Kay.

Because it would be stupid to park at the front door of the place they were planning to break into. Jamie hadn't given much thought to this part of the plan. She had been so focused on step one (get to the funeral home) and step three (see the body) that she had overlooked step two (get inside the building). Keeping their getaway vehicle out of sight made sense. Nick was right.

Jamie started to drive again with Benji hanging out the open door.

"Hey, you shits!" he barked. "Don't leave me!"

Jamie hit the brakes.

"Get in the car," Nick ordered.

Benji held onto the door and poked his head in. "You were gonna leave without me. I can't believe it. I should leave all of you!"

Kay twisted around. "Come on, Benji. Don't be like that."

"Yeah, get your ass in here," Nick hissed. "Don't make a scene."

Benji looked over his shoulder, but not another soul

was around. The funeral home was smack-dab in the industrial part of town, and all the surrounding businesses were closed for the night. The empty darkness of the lot added to the oppressive feeling that *they shouldn't be here.*

"Let's go," said Jamie.

Benji jumped in and slammed the door. "Fine," he mumbled, as if he had any say.

* * *

At the back of the building, Jamie parked the RAV behind a Dumpster and killed the engine. Everyone sat quietly, except for Benji, whose goddamn knee jittered up and down.

Jamie gulped, staring at the funeral home's steel door and electronic keypad system. She was in over her head.

What was I thinking? I'd just walk up to the door and knock? Stupid.

"So what now?" asked sweet, innocent Kay. "Is the manager going to let us in?"

Jamie gave her a side-eyed glance. "Maybe you better stay here."

"Why?"

"Because I don't think it's a good idea."

"Why? Because I'm in a wheelchair?"

"No, that's not what I— Look, I just don't think—" She stopped and closed her eyes, trying to collect her thoughts. "If we get caught—"

"This matters to me too."

"I know, but it was my idea. I'll go in." *Alone.* A chill raced up her back. *In a place where dead bodies are kept.*

"I wanna go too," said Benji. His door was open in an instant and he was almost halfway out again.

"Guys—"

"Please?" said Kay. "You can't just shut me out like the rest of the world."

"No one's shutting you out."

"You are! This happens to every person in a chair. You think it begins and ends with special parking, but it *doesn't*. We want the same opportunities."

Sighing, Nick eased in between their seats, laying a hand on Kay's headrest. His voice came on like a smooth vinyl record. "Even if that means looking at a dead guy?"

"Yes," she said, tilting her chin up and staring down her perfectly symmetrical nose.

Everything was perfect about Kay. She was as graceful and delicate as a butterfly — which was probably why Burt chose her.

"It's not gonna be pretty," Nick warned.

"I'll be fine." She opened her door and called Benji over. "Do you mind getting my chair for me, Benj? Please and thanks?"

"Of course," he said, and zipped around to the back of the RAV.

Jamie popped the trunk for him. As he struggled and swore, fighting to get the chair out, Jamie reached over Kay's lap and opened the glovebox. She grabbed a flashlight and a pair of leather gloves.

"What're those for?" Kay asked, tracing her fingers around her mouth.

She stole a glance at Nick. "For breaking and entering."

"Oh," whispered Kay.

"You sure you want to come?"

She nodded. "I have to."

Jamie watched Nick's hand drift down from the headrest and squeeze Kay's shoulder. They shared a grim smile, making Jamie feel like a third wheel in her own car. She climbed out, sticking the flashlight under her belt.

"You ready?" Benji opened Kay's door and helped her into her chair.

"Ready as I'll ever be," she said, with a shaky smile. "Thanks. You're a dear."

Benji shrugged, a fiery blush creeping up his neck and face. "I try."

Jamie rolled her eyes. *Are we done with the love fest?* "Let's do this."

Followed by the others, Jamie marched to the door as she slipped on her gloves. She tried the handle first, but of course the door was locked. Staring down the keypad, she was already out of her element.

As a teenager, the most criminal thing she had ever done (aside from nearly killing her stepfather) was to sneak out through the basement window to meet up with boys and drink beer in the park.

"Uhh…" She dared not look to the others for help. Their eyes burned into the back of her head, as they waited for her to lead them.

I don't know what I'm doing. We shouldn't be here. I'm not ready for this. Why did they listen to me?

"I got this."

Nick stepped up and she backed off. He crouched next to the keypad and pulled a piece of chalk from his pocket. He crushed it into a pile, which he swept into his palm. He held it in front of the keys and blew the chalk dust onto the pad.

Then he inspected the keys, tilting his head from side to side.

Jamie was sure she had seen this in a movie once. Something about the fingerprint oils left behind.

He stood up, dusted his hands on his pants and then pulled his shirt sleeve down to cover his hand. Using a covered knuckle, he punched in a code. The keypad light flashed green. There was a click. He grabbed the handle and—

"Voilà." He held the door open.

"Nice," said Benji, grinning. He went through first with Kay close behind.

Jamie lingered. "How did you do that?"

A slight smile tugged on the corner of Nick's lips. "Magic," he whispered, sending a shiver down her spine.

"No, really," she said. *So many questions.* "That pad's too new for anything to stick to it."

"Exactly. New enough that nobody's changed the universal presets yet… Blame it on my misspent youth."

Of course Nick had a rough childhood. He didn't talk about it much, but Jamie surmised his wayward teen behavior had been a major sticking point in his relationship with Burt.

He cocked his head back. "You going in or not?"

She stepped inside. As the door closed behind her, Nick wasn't there. "Aren't you coming?"

He shook his head. "Someone's gotta be the lookout."

Though she had thought she wanted to do it alone, she didn't like the idea of wandering around a funeral home after hours. Not alone, not with the others, not at all.

The only person she could imagine doing this mission

with wasn't even stepping inside the building.

Ice water churned in her gut, but she nodded, awkwardly giving him a salute. "See you soon."

He shut the door, leaving her in the dark.

CHAPTER 6

Jamie shuffled into the black nothingness where the door had been. Nick was gone. Message received. If he was attracted to or cared about her in any way, he would want to be with her. He wouldn't let her go alone.

She shivered, fumbling for her flashlight, when something clomped into her path. She turned the light on just as the large presence took it from her.

"Bloody Christ," muttered Benji, holding the light under his face. He looked like a shadowy ghoul. "What took so damn long? Leavin' us standing here like sittin' ducks."

Kay rolled down the hallway. "Where's Nick?"

"Playing lookout," she said.

"Chicken," Benji sneered. He squeezed around Kay in the narrow space and started flashing light on the doors. "So where do we go?"

Again, uncertainty struck Jamie. She pointed vaguely down the hall as they walked. She didn't know what she was going to do if they came to another locked door, especially with Nick no longer in their party.

"I think we need to find where they keep the bodies," said Kay.

Jamie rubbed her arms. *This is really happening.*

The funeral home wasn't very large and when they reached the end of the hall, they exited into the main parlor. A thick oriental rug covered the laminate wood floor. A small table held a bouquet of fresh-cut roses in an ornate vase, with two high-back chairs spaced out on either side.

Jamie recalled slouching in one in a different funeral home as she waited for her father's service to begin, drawing on a pamphlet she found about the stages of grief.

She never really knew the man. Tanner Riley left when she was young, and he usually weaseled out of his weekend custody arrangements to run off with a new girlfriend or play a gig.

One weekend, after he promised for weeks that he was going to take her to see a movie, he just didn't show. Surprise, surprise. Jamie pouted and ripped up the only photo she had of him.

A week later, people started calling the house. *Have you seen Tanner?* His latest girlfriend, his mom, the police — all asking Christine if she had heard anything. *Where would he go? It isn't like him to just disappear.*

But in Jamie's experience, disappearing was exactly like him. Tanner was unreliable and uncommunicative. He was selfish and immature. And he wasn't father material. He spent the night of her birth getting drunk in a dive bar. Though she didn't begrudge him any of those characteristics, she became apathetic about his existence.

After Burt ran off, the truth about what happened to her father came to light. Tanner's car had been sideswiped off a backcountry road. He spun out of control and veered off the road, disappearing down a steep embankment. Thick, undisturbed foliage swallowed him up. Tanner died on impact. His body wasn't found until weeks after Burt tried killing Jamie and Christine.

Jamie pressed her gloved hands together to stop them from trembling.

"This isn't it," whispered Kay. "Don't they usually keep bodies in, like, a freezer?"

Benji grunted, leading them back down the hallway. This time he tried opening every door they passed. The first two were offices, locked. The next was Embalming Room 1. The three exchanged a look as Benji gripped the handle.

"Here we go…" *Click, click.*

Locked.

He threw his shoulder into it, but the door refused to budge, and his show of strength didn't make it any less locked. "Shit… Anyone know how to pick a lock?"

Just forget it, Jamie wanted to say, but her younger self would have thrown a fit. *Find him. Make sure he's dead. Don't let him get away again.*

She looked down the hall. Embalming Room 2 was next. "What about that one?" She pointed.

Sighing, Benji shrugged. "Probably gonna be locked too."

Jamie couldn't leave without being sure. She pressed down on the handle and with a sharp click, the door opened. The hinges squeaked.

Benji held up the flashlight. "Holy shit. It worked."

None of this matters if he's not here.

Jamie went in first with Kay close behind. Benji stood in the doorway, swinging the flashlight's beam around in a futile attempt to ward off shadows.

Embalming Room 2 looked like a small medical office. Plain white cupboards formed an L-shape against the back half of the room, and the counter included a sink. A rolling tray table holding tools and equipment had been neatly tucked out of the way against the wall. Though everything looked clean and tidy, the room reeked of chemicals and rot.

Right dead center in the room, a body laid out on a stainless steel gurney.

It was Burt.

His skin appeared waxy and discolored, and without his outdated glasses, he almost looked like a completely different person.

But Jamie would know him anywhere.

Kay rolled closer, craning her neck for a better look. No one said a thing as they gathered around.

Jamie heard only her pulse pounding in her ears; not being able to hear if anyone was coming added to her growing anxiety of being in the same room as the monster who hurt her mother and killed her father. Who tried to kill her too.

Call me Daddy.

Benji sniffed, blinking too much. "Goddamn. Looks like he's about to get pointed."

"Hmm?" Kay asked.

"Remember that dumb fuckin' hobby of his?"

Jamie remembered. The pins. The specimen jars. The beautiful, dead creatures.

"Oh, right," said Kay. "Collecting butterflies."

"More like stabbing the poor bastards and puttin' them on display."

Just like he collected families.

Jamie reached out to touch him. She had to make sure it was really Burt, that it was an actual dead body, and not some dummy or blow-up doll — and that it wasn't all some sick dream she was about to wake up from.

Benji grabbed her hand and she gasped. "What're you doing?"

"Don't touch me," she snapped, shaking him off.

"Don't touch *him.*"

"Why the hell not?"

"Because it's gross."

"I have to check."

Jamie pushed him away. He stumbled against the counter and threw his hands up. "Fine. Do it then."

She planted herself next to Burt and tapped his arm. Her fingers grazed his cold, stiff body. Goosebumps broke out all over her skin and she stepped back as Kay wheeled in close enough to bang against the gurney. The metal on metal echoed throughout the room.

"Kay," Jamie warned.

Kay pushed herself up in her chair. Her pretty face twisted in anguish as she spat on the corpse. The gob landed on his cheek. *"Fuck you!"* Arms shaking, she collapsed back down in her chair. No one said a thing as she began to weep.

Stunned, Jamie backed away. She wanted to comfort her but didn't know how.

Benji stepped up and kicked the gurney. *"Fuck you, you son of a bitch!"*

Kay peeked through her fingers, watching Benji punch the body. His fists made meaty slapping sounds. He panted and swore, emitting heat.

Kay grabbed Benji's arm, stopping him. Wild-eyed, he whirled on her. Then, as if reading her mind, he slipped an arm around her dainty waist and hoisted her up, holding her over the body so she could throw her own punches.

When she ran out of steam, she slumped in Benji's arms and let out a primal scream. *"You took everything from me! Everything! I hate you!"*

Benji spat on him. "Fucking asshole!"

Jamie backed against the wall. Fire pumped through her veins. Their collective hate and anger stirred up her own.

For years, she lived in fear, never knowing where he had gone or if he was planning his revenge. Even after Nick stopped him, even after an intense trial, even after he was thrown in prison, she still feared that she would feel Burt's breath on her face late one night.

Fingers throbbing, she blindly snatched a tool off the tray table. With a strangled cry, she charged toward the gurney, pushing past the others. Hand raised above her head, she stabbed Burt.

The scalpel jutted out of his chest.

Nausea and guilt overtook her rage. She stared at her trembling hands.

I can't believe I did that... She pushed herself away from the gurney. *I need air. I need to get out of here.*

Beads of blood bubbled up around the scalpel. Burt's

chest sagged. His jaw dropped, releasing a rancid puff of air. His sudden gasp took their breaths away.

Kay held onto Benji, who guided her away from the gurney and set her back down in her chair. "Jesus Christ," he breathed.

The door flew open and they shrieked.

"What the fuck?" cried Nick, seeing the scalpel in Burt's chest.

"Wh-what're you—?" Jamie's tongue was as thick as lead.

"I heard you screaming from outside, you morons," he said through gritted teeth. *"We gotta go."*

She wiped her brow, trying to compose herself. "No, we need to clean up. Make sure—"

"There's no time," he snapped, pushing Kay and her wheelchair out of the room. "We gotta go now — *someone's here."*

CHAPTER 7

They left the room as it was, which wasn't much different than the way they had found it — except for the scalpel sticking out of the corpse in the middle of the room and DNA evidence splattered all over.

All of these thoughts raced through Jamie's mind as they fled the embalming room, but there was a much worse thought she couldn't shake.

As they reached the back door, she tapped Nick's shoulder.

Pushing Kay to the door, he jerked his neck around to glare at Jamie. *"What?"*

"We can't— He's still alive."

Kay looked up at Nick. Her hand reached up and curled around his wrist. "We have to go," she begged. "I don't want to get in trouble."

"We're already in trouble!" Jamie pointed back the way they had come. "You saw it! Burt's *alive!*"

"We gotta go," said Benji. "If I miss work tomorrow, I'm toast."

Jamie spun around on him. "You're not gonna *have a tomorrow* unless we do something about—"

Nick grabbed her arm. *"Stop it."* Again, he didn't raise his voice, but his words were loud and clear. He held her close enough that even though his voice simmered with rage, she wanted to run her fingers through that tempting strand of hair that hung off the side of his face. "Have you never seen a dead person before?"

She stammered — but the truth was she had not. Her father's funeral had been closed casket. Someone at the ceremony said something about Burt Mengle "doing a real number on the guy."

I never got to see him. I never got to say goodbye.

She turned to look over her shoulder, expecting to see her stepfather lurking behind them to crack wise: *"Well then, Jelly Bean, lemme help ya say hello now — in Hell!"*

Nick snapped his fingers in her face. Her arm felt cold where his hand had been.

"Burt moved," she said.

"It's a spasm," he said. "Rigor mortis. Happens to all of 'em."

She didn't want to know how he knew that. *Blame it on my misspent youth.*

"I—" She was going to stand her ground and argue, but a light flashed behind them. Suddenly convinced, she seized Nick's jacket, urging him to lead them through the dark and out of this horrible place.

He turned to Kay, taking control of her wheelchair, and raced for the back exit. Benji stampeded, pushing Jamie forward. A beam of light fell on them.

She dared to look behind.

The light hit her face, blinding her. She bumped against Nick and was sandwiched by Benji, scraping at her heels. She yelped.

Benji gave her a shove. *"Come on! Move it!"*

At the end of the hallway, Nick stopped short. Kay threw her hands out in front to stop from flying at the door. Nick skirted her aside and kicked the door open.

The group hustled out of the building and into the parking lot, bolting for the RAV.

As the funeral home door slammed behind them, Nick barked orders. "Gimme the keys. Benji, take Kay. Jamie, help me with the chair."

They each did their part. There was no time to argue. Jamie tossed the keys to Nick. Benji lifted Kay out of the chair and once Nick unlocked the door, he helped her into the front seat. Then he helped Nick and Jamie jam the chair in the back. It was harder than before with the time crunch. Finally, Benji roared and rammed his shoulder against the rear door until the lock caught.

Jamie held out her hand for her keys. A tremor rippled through her fingers. Nick saw it too. He opened the back door for her. "I'll drive," he said. She opened her mouth to protest, but he shot her an intense look. "Don't fight me on this."

She jumped in the back with Benji, twisting around in her seat as Nick peeled out of the back alley. A wood-paneled station wagon that hadn't been there before was parked in front of the building. It was hard to catch any details as her eyes adjusted.

Is there someone in the car? Are they watching us? She wondered if the driver had seen her car, if they had taken down her license plate number. *Did they see us?*

As a cold feeling sank down in her gut, she grabbed her seatbelt, fingers worrying the fabric.

Did we wake Burt?

CHAPTER 8

By Monday, Jamie had chewed her fingernails down to the quick. Nail biting wasn't one of her usual nervous habits, but without work coming in, she didn't have anything to keep her busy.

So when Kay called, Jamie was staring at ten nubby, sore fingers.

"Are we going to get caught?" Kay asked before saying hello. That definitely wasn't like her. She was so unfailingly polite that what happened the previous week must have been eating her alive in the same way that Jamie was gnawing away at herself.

"I don't know," she admitted.

"I-I think we should tell Dr. Henshaw."

Jamie was glad she was sitting down because Kay's words made the floor disappear from under her office chair. The walls tilted. She bent over and put her head between her knees, waiting for the dizzy spell to subside.

Another dizzy spell. The third one since they fled the funeral home. *What's wrong with me?*

"Don't," she grunted as blood rushed to her head.

"Why? I need to tell someone."

"Tell *me* then."

"You're not my therapist. And you already know what happened."

"Yeah, but you can't tell Dr. H. or we'll all be in trouble."

"What about doctor/patient confidentiality?"

"I don't think that covers crimes."

"I don't like this…"

"Look, if she brings it up, fine. We'll discuss it then, but she'll probably guilt trip us into going to the police."

Kay was silent for a moment. "Maybe I *want* to go to the police."

Jamie covered her mouth, drawing a deep breath. "Did you talk to the guys?"

"Well, no," she said. "It was your idea, so…"

My idea. Her fingers traveled up to her forehead, rubbing the spot above her eye where a pulse started beating. It pumped every time she thought about all the ways *her idea* was going to bite her in the ass. The worst part was that breaking into the funeral home hadn't brought any closure. *Burt gasped.* She needed to go back and make sure he was dead.

He should be dead. I stabbed him in the heart.

How can I be so sure? I'm a graphic designer — not an anatomy expert.

Nick said it was normal rigor mortis stuff. *Everything is fine.*

Everything is not fine.

Before she could make up an excuse to keep Kay quiet, another call interrupted. She checked the screen and saw Henshaw's name. *Speak of the devil.* "Damn."

"What?"

"I have to go," she said. "Promise me you won't say anything just yet?"

"I don't know…"

"Please?"

"I—"

"I'll talk to you later." She hung up on Kay and switched over to Henshaw. Her leg bounced around like Benji's. Forcing herself to stop, she said, "Hey, Dr. H. What's up?"

"Hi, Jamie. I'm afraid I have some unsettling news."

Jamie's first thought was to hang up the phone. She didn't want to hear about her mistakes and poor choices. If she did, she could call her mother more often.

Henshaw's "unsettling" news could wait until tomorrow's group session. And if the police wanted to arrest her, they could come and get her. She refused to be threatened with surveillance footage of herself leading a pack of disgruntled and broken victims into a locked building to violate a corpse.

We — I — mutilated his body.

He's going to be pissed.

Shut up. He's not alive. Stop it.

She laughed nervously, holding back her percolating anxiety. "What else is new?" She meant it as a joke, but it came out flat.

"I hope you're sitting down," advised Henshaw.

"I'm sitting."

"Burt Mengle's body, uh… How do I put this?"

I'm so screwed.

She swallowed again. Her throat constricted. There wasn't enough moisture in her mouth to clear the lump in her throat. Her hand and brain crossed signals and she reached suddenly for her water glass, but her knuckles hit the side of it. It toppled over, splashing her wall and crashing to the floor.

"Burt's body is missing."

CHAPTER 9

Jamie jumped up, hitting her head on the underside of her desk. The knock was hard enough to black out her vision with flashing shapes. She slumped back down, rubbing her head. When she looked up, a man's shadow fell across her doorway.

Burt.

I was right.

Now I'm dead.

Dr. Henshaw continued talking. "I don't want you to concern yourself with this matter, because it's simply a miscommunication between the prison and the funeral home. I have one more appointment this afternoon and then I'm on my way to speak to someone about this. I'll let you know everything I find out at tomorrow's session."

Jamie scrambled out from under her desk. As her vision returned, the shadow disappeared. It was only a figment of her imagination. No one was there.

"Are you alright, Jamie?"

She stammered out an affirmative answer as she swept through the rest of her apartment, checking to make sure her home was clear. The balcony door was secure and the front door remained locked and chained.

"Good," Henshaw said. "There's something else I need to tell you and the others, but it can wait until tomorrow."

"Okay," Jamie agreed, eager to end the call.

"Please take care and be sure to call the emergency line if this news gives you any difficulties. I'll see you tomorrow."

By mid-afternoon the next day, as Jamie mulled over what to wear in case Henshaw interrogated them about their reckless, destructive, criminal behavior, she got a phone call from the appointment booking service.

Henshaw had not shown up for any of her appointments and the group session that night had to be canceled.

"We'll call back to rebook once we hear from Dr. Henshaw."

Jamie was relieved. A week's reprieve from having to face the others and the consequences of their actions.

But by the weekend, no one had called to rebook the session. Jamie was almost tempted to call Kay to see if she heard anything. She changed her mind, thinking that she didn't want to be the one to remind Kay about what happened at the funeral home.

Instead, she tried calling her mom again. Her rent was about to go up, and though she could scrape together enough for the first month, she would be broke by Christmas.

Again, her mother's voicemail blocked her. After the

beep, she groaned. "Mom! Come on! I need to talk. Where are you?" She paused, as if waiting for her mom to pick up. "Look, I need... I need money, okay? Call me back?"

Waiting, she stared at the phone in her hand for five minutes. Then she looked around at the walls of her apartment. She wanted to hate this space — the cheap kitchen cupboards and the peeling linoleum, the balcony door that never latched properly, the weird stain glass art on her bathroom window. As soon as she received the notice about the rent increase, she began telling herself that the apartment was a shithole.

But it hadn't been a shithole when she first found it. It hadn't been a shithole when she set up her home office, or when she began a little herb garden in the kitchen window, or when she opened the balcony one summer morning and smelled the ocean air off Kitsilano Beach.

She loved her apartment. After bouncing from rental to rental for the past decade, she finally found a home that made her feel as safe as her old house in Mary Hill. She missed that place, and for the rest of the day, it was all she could think about. *You can't go home again.*

Yeah, but I can drive past it for a look.

As soon as that thought entered her brain, she got in her car and drove. She wasn't thinking about Henshaw or Kay or Burt. She just wanted to go home.

By the time she pulled onto Pitt River Road, the sun had set and the streetlights came to life. A few people were walking their dogs. A jogger ran past, eyeing her vehicle suspiciously. Jamie turned on her dome light to show that she was not there to "case" any houses.

Don't worry — I only break into funeral homes.

The house was a two-level split wedged into a hill. The

top half was covered in white stucco; the bottom half had worn green siding. Tall trees walled off the house from its neighbors, muffling any sounds.

A FOR SALE sign protruded from the lawn. Jamie mused on what it would cost to buy it back, make it her own. *Take it back from that horrible memory.* Would it still have the shaggy pink carpeting in the master bedroom? Would it still have the pink bathroom set? Would the kitchen still feel cramped with all the dark wood cabinets?

The porch light flickered on. Jamie gasped. The front door opened — *and Burt stepped out.* He gave her a friendly wave.

She crouched down, fumbling with her keys. Burt sauntered down the curved driveway toward her car. The RAV's engine betrayed her, emitting a whine and refusing to turn over. There was no escape.

And then he tapped on the passenger side window. A scream bubbled up, catching in her throat. She turned to face him and—

It wasn't Burt.

Of course it's not Burt, for fuck's sake.

The man motioned for her to roll down the window. Still on high alert, she cracked it the slightest bit and forced a shaky smile.

"Hi there," said the man. Wearing a tailored gray suit and a blue tie, he had the widest smile she had ever seen. His thick-framed glasses slid down his nose as he leaned in. His fingers curled over the edge of the window.

"Y-yes?" Shaking, she didn't know what to do.

"If you're interested in the house, I can show you around," he said.

"I'm sorry?" Was he offering to let a stranger into his house?

Her finger twitched on the power window button, but she couldn't overcome the nagging need to be polite *(be a good girl, Jelly Bean)* and shut the window.

Who's Daddy's good girl?

"This is a pretty hot neighborhood," he said, reaching into his blazer. *He has a gun!* It was too dark to be sure.

"No, please—"

As he withdrew his hand, she hit the button. The window rolled up, separating them — though she still had nowhere to go. The car wouldn't start.

At the last second, he stuck a slip of paper through. A business card fluttered onto the passenger seat. "That's my card," he said. "I'd love to help you find your way home."

She picked up the card. *Kelly Fiero.* So he wasn't a deranged lunatic out to get her. Just a real estate agent.

"I was just about to lock up for the night," he explained. "But I can still give you a tour."

The adrenaline pounding in her head subsided. She rubbed her eyes and laughed nervously. "No, I... I used to live here."

He glanced over his shoulder and smiled. "No kidding."

She nodded, rolling the window back down a little more. "Yeah, a few years ago."

"And I bet you drive past it all the time."

Blushing, she shrugged. "Sometimes."

He chuckled. "You'd be surprised how often people do that. You always miss what you used to have."

"I guess so."

"Hey…" He grinned. "You really can go have a look. But only if you want."

A cool breeze whispered across the back of her neck, like Burt's cold, dead fingers grasping for a handful of her once long, black hair. "I don't know…"

He checked his watch. "Tick tock. This could be your last chance to look around… See your old room…"

She stared longingly at the old house, imagining the plush carpet between her toes and bounding upstairs to her bedroom.

But the only light on was the porchlight. The rest of the house was black. What kind of open house was held in the dark?

Besides, she knew better than to enter an empty house with a strange man.

She shook her head. "No, I can't."

"Are you sure?" He raised an eyebrow. "Last chance. Come on…"

"It's not… It's gonna be different and I don't think I can handle that right now." She tried the ignition again, pumping the gas pedal. This time the RAV roared to life.

The man frowned as another jogger trotted past, watching them curiously. "Too bad. Well, you've got my card, so if you need anything, give me a shout."

He trudged back up to the house, giving her a wave as she peeled off from the curb. Only when she was a few blocks away did the tension in her shoulders begin to recede, followed by a jolt of anger.

Stupid! She bashed her hands on the steering wheel and berated herself. *What was I thinking? I shouldn't have come out here.*

Then she started to cry. That had been her only chance

to see the house again and she let a boring man in a suit scare her away, and soon someone else would move in and bury the rest of her childhood memories (the good ones, at least) under cheap paint and trendy furnishings.

It's not my house anymore. It's not my home.

You can't go home again.

CHAPTER 10

Group therapy resumed the following week with one major difference: Dr. Henshaw was not there.

Neither was Nick, but that was not surprising.

Jamie sat in her usual spot, hands clasped between her knees as she waited anxiously for Kay to squeal about the funeral home and what they did to Burt's body.

His missing body.

She shivered, drawing Benji's attention. "You cold?"

"No." She shook her head.

"You thinking about…?" He clicked his tongue.

"No," she lied.

Instead of Henshaw, a barrel-chested man in his early fifties entered the room. One hell of an ugly sweater vest clung to his bulging stomach, and with it, he paired pleated khakis and brown loafers. His short beard was speckled with silver hairs, and his gray eyes crinkled when he smiled. He looked like the dad in an old sitcom.

"Hi, everybody," he said, reading their names on his clipboard. "Let's see… We're missing someone."

"Nick Michaels," Kay said. "He isn't here." Then she pointed at the others as she introduced them. "… And I'm Kay Quigley. Though it probably says Karolyn on your sheet."

"Yes, Karolyn…" He peered down his nose through his bifocals, giving Jamie a sudden image of Burt staring down his nose at a painting she brought home from art class: A cockroach crawling out of a cracked skull.

"I'm gonna put it in my portfolio," she told her mom. "Mrs. Richter thinks I could get into Emily Carr, but I have to start putting some pieces together now."

Burt adjusted his glasses, like it was his vision preventing him from appreciating her hard work and budding talent. "Emily Carr? Art school? I don't know…"

Christine placed a hand on his arm. "Now Burt…"

"No, I know," he said, stepping back. "I just think spending money on an artsy-fartsy school is a bit frivolous. Post-secondary education is very expensive, and you want to throw my money away on art school? *In* this *economy?"*

"I don't want your money," she snapped. She yanked the painting out of his hands and stormed off to her room. Fuck him.

She repressed the anger that surfaced as Henshaw's replacement introduced himself. Something about him reminded her of Burt. She tried reading the others' faces for their reactions, but even Benji was uncharacteristically placid.

"Think of me as a *substitute* psychotherapist," he said. "My name is Dr. Brewster, and I have over twenty years' experience in the area of group therapy. My job is to facilitate discussions and—"

"Where's Dr. Henshaw?" Kay interrupted.

Narrowing her eyes, Jamie glanced at her. *She's just dying to rat me out.*

Brewster's eyebrows lifted in surprise. If he wasn't used to being interrupted, he was in for a rude awakening from this group.

"I'm not at liberty to say."

"What do you mean?" Kay asked.

Benji scoffed. "Means he doesn't know."

"She's our therapist," said Kay. "We have a right to know."

Brewster rubbed his beard, considering the group. He was hard to read behind his thick-lensed glasses, but at last he broke with a sigh.

"It's a private matter at the moment," he said. "But I can understand how it might be difficult for our discussions to go any farther, so here it is: Dr. Henshaw is missing."

* * *

After a question period that went around in circles and ate up the hour, Dr. Brewster asked if anyone felt like disbanding or suspending the group sessions until Dr. Henshaw returned. Jamie, Benji, and Kay gave non-committal answers and then opted to end the session early to think about it.

They drifted out into the parking lot. Benji was already on his phone searching for news about their missing therapist. Nothing yet, so he made a big show of creating a Google Alert.

"This way I'll be the first to know."

I doubt that, thought Jamie, staring across the lot at her car. Under the orange streetlight, raindrops glistened on the hood and windshield.

"If no one's heard from her since last week," wondered Kay, "what do you think happened?"

"She called me," Jamie blurted out. "Last Monday."

"Did she tell you anything?" Kay moved in, as if her presence could compel Jamie to spill the details.

Gripping her keys, Jamie desperately wanted to get inside her vehicle. "She said Burt's body disappeared."

"What?!" they both cried.

Benji grabbed his head, pacing back and forth. "Are you fucking kidding me?"

"This better not be a joke," warned Kay.

"When have you ever known me to make a joke?" she shot back. "She called me. It's the truth."

"Why would she tell you and not us?"

"I don't know." She shrugged. "She likes me best?"

Kay wrinkled her nose. "Now *that* sounds like a joke."

"I really don't know. Maybe because I suggested he could still be alive? She told me not to be concerned. She was gonna figure it out."

Benji froze, hands still on his head. "Wait. You don't think the missing body has something to do with Dr. H. missing, do you?"

That dizzy feeling threatened to topple Jamie again. She used the RAV as a grounding point, leaning against it with her arms crossed. "What am I, a detective?"

"No, no, no," he said. "There's gotta be a reasonable explanation."

Kay looked over her shoulder. "I don't like this."

"Me neither," said Jamie.

"I think we should tell Nick."

"What's the point?" said Benji. "He's just gonna say what we all know — bodies don't just up and walk away."

"They don't," Jamie agreed quietly, if only to vocalize that fact for herself.

"And he's not even here *now*. So clearly, he doesn't give a shit."

"He probably doesn't know," she said.

Benji threw his arms up and started pacing again. "Oh, jeez, sorry! I forgot I'm talking to the Team Nick Fan Club! Christ. Hell, I'm an attractive young man with a troubled past too, ya know."

Jamie blushed, turning away so they couldn't see. It was no secret that Kay was sweet on Nick, but Jamie preferred to keep her own pathetic crush hidden. She was pushing thirty — it was silly to have immature feelings for another messed-up headcase.

"So what then? We wait around until Dr. Henshaw turns up?" asked Kay.

"Or the body? Or *Henshaw's* body?" asked Benji.

Their questions made Jamie's head spin. She staggered around and opened her door. "I'll deal with it," she said. "I-I'll call Nick. I'll find out about the body. Just … be careful."

They stared after her. Warning them was unnecessary. They too had lived through this nightmare before.

CHAPTER 11

Back at her apartment building, Jamie paused at the mailboxes. She stuck her key in her lockbox, scrolling through her phone contacts to find Nick's number. She had never called him before, not even to confirm if a session was postponed or if one of them was considering skipping that week. She had saved his number for something important. She didn't want to bother him with trivial chit chat.

Henshaw missing was anything but trivial.

Her thumb hesitated over his name.

He needs to know.

Know what? I don't know anything.

Not ready to make that call, she dropped the phone into her bag. *I'll call him after I get the mail...* And then once she was settled and secure in her apartment, she would give him a call.

Sorting through the letters and flyers that had

accumulated in the mailbox since she last checked, she flipped over a red envelope. *JAMIE.*

No return address. It had to have been hand delivered.

She envisioned another "friendly" reminder from her landlord about the upcoming rent increase. She paused near the stairs to pry open the envelope.

Inside was a greeting card. A swirl of flowers and rainbows adorned the front.

MISS YOU.

She scratched her landlord off the list of potential admirers. The only person who would possibly miss her was her mom, but even she had run off to the opposite side of the continent.

Jamie's eyes watered as she opened it. Hoping for an act of motherly reconciliation, she found darkness.

Scrawled after a cursive poem about family and love and all that bullshit was a signature.

LOVE, DADDY.

Jamie's breath caught in her throat. She tried sucking more in, but the more she tried, the tighter her throat felt. Then her heart stopped. The world around her stopped. She was sinking into that overwhelming dizziness and tried to grab onto the wall for support, but it slid out from under her and she was crashing to the ground. There was no way she could make it upstairs to her second-floor unit.

Need help. Call 911. I'm having a heart attack.

Unable to call out, she fumbled for her phone. She dumped the contents of her bag onto the floor until she spotted her phone among the litter of receipts, compact mirrors, and used lip balm. She picked it up, dialing the first number on her screen.

Nick's groggy voice came on the line. "Hey. Jamie?"

She couldn't speak. Gasping for breath, she was drowning in a panic attack — and accidentally calling Nick compounded her anxiety.

"Are you okay? What's going on?"

"Burt..." she wheezed. "H-he's gone."

"No," he said. "He's not."

But Nick didn't know. Henshaw hadn't warned him — only Jamie. "His body's missing... And now Henshaw."

"Henshaw?"

"And... I... can't... *breathe.*"

"Okay, hang on."

He was quiet long enough that she thought he had left her. Calm new age music began playing in the background as he talked low and slowly. "You still there? Can you hear the music?"

She nodded, as if he could see her.

"Take a deep breath now. One..."

She clutched the phone, hand cramping, as she focused on his voice, on matching her breathing to his. His deep, steady voice guided her through the fog, and she could almost lift her head without the whole world spinning.

Calmer now, she sat up and began to collect her things. She kept the phone to her ear, soaking in the sound of Nick softly counting. Tingles spread out from her scalp and trickled down her spine.

He stopped. "You alright?"

"Yeah," she whispered. She cleared her throat of that husky, intimate tone and gathered herself. "I'm fine. I'm ... not fine."

"What happened?"

"It's a long story."

"I got time."

* * *

Nick stayed on the phone while Jamie got settled in her apartment. He didn't say much or ask any questions; just waited until she spread her mail across the coffee table. Bills, flyers, and the red envelope. The card stood upright, teasing her with a view of those handwritten words.

LOVE, DADDY.

She ran a hand through her choppy bangs. "I don't know where to start."

"How about when I last saw you?"

"At the—?" She stopped herself from saying it, wondering if someone could be listening in, or had bugged her phone. *Paranoia, the destroyer.* "Afterward nothing really happened. Except for Henshaw calling to say Burt's missing. So sometime between that Thursday and Monday, he just up and vanished."

"And then Henshaw vanished too?"

"Yeah. And so this new guy, Dr. Brewster? He says it's a private matter, so I don't know if that means the police are involved or what. But I remember Henshaw saying she was going to find out about the missing body, and then *she* goes missing. Isn't that weird?"

"And then you got a card in your mail today?"

"Did you get anything?"

"Don't know, haven't checked."

Jamie rubbed her eyes. "I should call the others. Let them know."

"It's probably just a stupid prank."

"But what if—?"

"Don't do that," he said. "Don't play what-ifs. He's gone. Dead. The funeral home messed up. That's all. Or they saw what…" *What you guys did to him.* "…What happened and decided to cover it up. He's probably in the ground already. Nothing to worry about."

"Yeah, maybe." Her hand traveled down her face until she could chomp down on her thumbnail. "But don't you think it's a weird coincidence that Henshaw—?"

He cut her off. "That's all it is. A coincidence."

She envied his confidence, his certainty, but she also wanted his trust. Burt had done this before. He made everyone think he was dead. No one believed her then — not until he did it three more times.

"I better go," she said. "But, um, thanks for, uh, talking me down."

"Any time," he said.

"See you at group next week?"

"Maybe."

CHAPTER 12

B y the following Tuesday, everyone but Nick and Dr. Brewster had received a card from "Daddy." Jamie, Benji, and Kay each set theirs down in the middle of the circle, so everyone could have a look and theorize what it all meant.

Sitting in Henshaw's usual spot, Brewster scratched his scruffy beard. "Could be a prank," he suggested.

"That's what I said," muttered Nick.

"Anybody got any lighter fluid?" asked Benji. "We should start a bonfire up in this bitch."

Ignoring Benji, Jamie pointed at the cards. "And Burt's missing body? Is that a prank too?"

"That must be something else," said Brewster. "A misunderstanding, perhaps."

"Misunderstandings and miscommunications! What if it's not?"

"What do you suppose?" he asked.

Benji groaned, drawing everyone's attention. "She thinks ol' Burt's a zombie and he's coming to eat our brains." He reached out his arms like a hungry ghoul and shook Jamie's shoulder.

She smacked his hand away. "Shut up."

Brewster blinked in surprise. "Really?"

"That's not what I'm saying. I think—" Everyone but Brewster knew what she thought, and she knew that they thought she was crazy. So she looked down at the three cards and left it at that. "I just think it's all kinda strange."

"Well, even if it is a prank," said Kay, clutching her tissues, "I'm scared. I used to get all sorts of weird phone calls after…"

Kay didn't need to say the words. They all understood. Jamie especially. She received the same calls not long after Burt ran off.

She and her mom were living with friends, struggling to get their lives back on track. Each night around nine o'clock someone would call from an unknown number. The caller wouldn't say anything, just breathed heavily, their nose whistling with each inhale.

She tried asking questions, making demands, yelling, cursing, crying, and begging him to stop, but the caller wouldn't say a word.

Though she couldn't prove it, she knew it was Burt. He was letting her know that she hadn't won. That *he* escaped, and he would make sure *she* never would.

"Your aunt's got an alarm system?" asked Nick. Kay nodded. "Better keep using it."

"Pfft," Benji spat. "Alarms don't do shit. Get a gun."

"No," she said. "Guns are awful." She turned to Nick.

"And I can't be in my house all the time. I don't want to live like a prisoner. *I* didn't do anything wrong! *I'm not the one who killed people.*"

"No one's saying you can't have a life," said Nick.

"Just be careful," said Jamie.

"I *am* careful. I just don't know how much longer I can live like this."

Everyone stared, waiting to see if she was going to confess a deep, dark desire to end it all.

"That's not what I'm saying," she said, reading the room. Her thumb and forefinger traced the outline of her lips. "I just want a normal life, that's all. Can we talk about something else? Please?"

Brewster tried steering the conversation to other things, but they kept circling back to Henshaw. He fiddled with his glasses each time they mentioned her name. His lips pinched together as he let them speak their peace and get their questions out into the open. With the way he fumbled through his answers, Jamie figured he knew about as much as they did.

Or he's hiding something.

As the rest of the evening's discussion droned on. Jamie tried to catch Nick's eye. She wanted to let him know that she wasn't embarrassed about accidentally calling him in the middle of a panic attack. But his inability — or unwillingness — to look in her direction suggested he was embarrassed for her. At least that's the lie her anxiety-riddled brain and overactive imagination told her.

He thinks I'm a freak.

He was just being nice.

By the time the session concluded, she decided she had

better say something to clear the air. She jumped out of her seat and hurried after him to the door.

She tapped his shoulder before he could get away. He turned around, eyebrows raised.

"Hey, uh, you have a second?" she asked.

"What's up?" He pulled on his jacket, moving toward the exit.

"I, uh, just wanted to thank you for, uh, taking my call last week." Her face warmed up. "It was an accident, of course, but..."

He shrugged. "No big deal. And hey, they'll find 'em, you know."

"Burt or Henshaw?"

He shrugged again, smiling sadly as he slipped out the door. Benji and Kay came up behind her. She scurried out after Nick, following him down the stairs. He glanced up at her as she swung through the stairwell door, but he didn't slow his pace.

It was like he was trying to avoid her, and she couldn't take the hint.

She quickened her pace, hoisting her bag up her shoulder. When she was close enough behind him, she tried continuing their conversation. "So, uh, what're you doing now?"

"Nothin'."

"Same," she said. "Nothin' going on for me either."

When they hit the main floor, it was her last chance. *Do it. Just ask him.*

The elevators dinged open. Kay and Benji strolled out, pausing to watch Jamie attempt something bold. It was the fastest that damn elevator had ever moved, and it screwed up Jamie's timing. Now she had an audience.

"So, uh, I was wondering something," she said to Nick, while trying to ignore their stares. "If you're not doing anything tonight and I'm not doing anything, and we're both not doing anything, I wonder if you want to get a drink? With me? There's a bar up the street that I heard—"

"No." He turned up his collar and headed for the exit.

"No, like, some other time? Or no, like—"

Pausing at the door, he turned with a sigh. "Just *no.*"

"Oh, well, that's…" She wanted to say something cool and carefree. *Whatever. No big deal. Catch ya on the flipside.* Maybe not that last one. But he was gone.

Kay and Benji inched past her, muttering goodnight as they left.

Skin crawling with embarrassment, Jamie waited until they were out of sight before she pushed the door handle to leave.

Behind her, Dr. Brewster cleared his throat. "Jamie? You left something behind."

Now what? she thought miserably.

When she turned around, Brewster was suddenly too close. He towered over her. For a big man, he moved fast.

The light above flickered, threatening to blanket them in darkness.

Jamie pushed back against the door, staring into his narrowed eyes magnified behind his thick lenses. She almost didn't see what he was holding until he forced it into her hands.

Her fingers grazed the sharp edges.

"You forgot your card."

CHAPTER 13

B rewster couldn't have been more wrong. *It's not mine, I didn't forget it, and I don't want it.*

Stuffing the card in her bag, Jamie tried to laugh off her forgetfulness and fear.

"What's troubling you?" Brewster asked, standing too close. His coffee breath wafted against her face.

"Nothing," she said, forcing a smile. "I need to get home and—"

Kay's Aunt Krystal arrived, honking the minivan's horn. She barked at Kay to hurry up. Jamie made a mental note to check in with Kay tomorrow.

Brewster's hand grazed her back, brushing across her bra strap. The hairs on the back of her neck began to rise.

"Jamie," he said. "I can take you on if you need extra help."

"Extra help?" she gulped.

"Losing Dr. Henshaw is clearly troubling you, so I

want you to know that I'm here for you."

"We haven't *lost* Dr. Henshaw," she said, sharply. "She's *missing." Unless you know something we don't.*

"Of course, of course," he replied. "But for the time being, she's not with us, and that may be causing some distress for you and the other members of the group."

"I'm fine."

"As long as you're certain," he said, stepping back. "You can change your mind. I'm here for you any time."

"What about Kay? After what she said tonight? What if she hurts herself?"

He scratched his beard. "Don't worry. I'll make sure she's taken care of."

Jamie didn't bother saying goodbye. She slipped out the door, looking around for the others. Aunt Krystal's minivan and Kay drove away. The only cars left were the RAV and a silver sedan that probably belonged to Brewster.

The parking lot was darker than normal tonight. The light she parked under was dead, and shadows filled her car. Aside from the traffic sounds from the next street over, it was deathly quiet.

She fumbled around in her bag for her keys, trying to keep an eye out for muggers or carjackers or worse — Burt Mengle's pale corpse shambling toward her, a bloody scalpel dangling out of his chest, his arms outstretched to strangle her — when the office door banged shut.

She jumped, clamping down on a shriek. But it was only Dr. Brewster, locking up for the night. Tucking the keys in his pocket, he strolled after her.

And then he began to whistle.

A chill ran down Jamie's back. Old memories re-surfaced. Burt coming home from work, whistling "My Bonnie Lies over the Ocean." Burt stabbing needles and pins through dead butterflies and spreading their wings open. Burt marching upstairs in the Mary Hill house to kill her.

She quickened her pace and rushed to the RAV. Her key scratched the paint as she struggled to get it in the lock. Brewster was almost upon her. The lock clicked. She threw the door open and dove inside, slamming the door — just as he passed by, giving her a friendly wave.

Only when he got in his own car and drove away did Jamie release her breath.

* * *

Bad dreams disrupted Jamie's sleep: Corpses crawled out of the earth and chased her through an empty parking lot. Disembodied hands reached out of a never-ending staircase to grab her. Nick constricted her in a hot and heavy embrace, blood oozing out of his mouth and eyeballs, before melting into the shape of Dr. Brewster.

Only a loud, pulsing beat woke her, releasing her from the nightmares.

She cracked her sore, heavy eyes open and reached for her phone. "Fuck," she groaned, realizing she had snoozed through her alarm half a dozen times.

No, what woke her was the phone's ring. She didn't recognize the number on the screen. She considered ignoring it or sending it to voicemail, but a hopeful part of her thought it might be a potential client. Or better yet, a past client with a load of money and an easy assignment.

So she answered it.

At first the person on the other end didn't say anything, and she was taken back to the months following Burt's escape. The heavy breather with the nose whistle, taunting her. Now the breather was back.

She was paralyzed — until the caller sniffled.

"Is this Jamie?" asked a woman, voice cracking.

"Uh, yeah." She rubbed her eyes, relieved that it wasn't Burt. *He's dead. Stop thinking otherwise.* "That's me."

"Um… This is Krystal Quigley, Kay's aunt."

She sat up suddenly. "Hi. What's going on?" She had never in her life talked to Aunt Krystal. *Something is wrong.*

"I'm just wondering if Kay said anything in the group session last night?"

Kay said a lot of things. "Why?"

"I know it's supposed to be confidential and all that, but… I need to know." Krystal gulped. "Because, um… Kay took her life last night."

Jamie's throat tightened. Her hand flew reflexively to her mouth, but she made no other movements. Time stopped.

* * *

"Sweeeeeeet Caroline! BOM BOM BOM!"

Each limping stomp of his foot as he circled Kay, his knife dripping with blood. Her mother Lori's mangled body slumped in the bathtub. Kay dragged herself on her stomach, by her elbows. The carpet burned her forearms, but not her legs.

Why can't I feel my legs? Her mom's bathroom was too pink, the blood mixing with the bath water was too pink. Too pink.

"I liked him," Kay admitted early in their group sessions. "He seemed really nice and he liked my mom a lot. Even brought me my own flower whenever he brought my mom a bouquet. I didn't think there was anything wrong. I didn't know… And then it was too late."

Too late. The tides of turmoil within Burt changed, and Kay spent the rest of her life scrutinizing what had gone wrong. *Didn't he like them? Wasn't her mother head over heels in love with her new husband? Wasn't she the perfect daughter?*

What she didn't know then was that while mulling over his life's decisions as he stabbed pins through a butterfly's thorax, Burt came to the realization that he no longer wanted a daughter. Girls meant trouble. When boys came sniffing around, girls' love for their fathers lessened. Disappeared. He'd had trouble with daughters before, starting with Jamie. Perhaps even with his first daughter. After a while, they stopped being faithful to their daddies. But a son… Even a troubled young man like Nick or a brood of rambunctious boys like Benji and his brothers were more to Burt's liking.

Kay dragged herself out of her mother's room and to the staircase. Then as Burt swooped in for his final attack, she hurled herself down the stairs, landing in a crumpled pile at the front door. Arm broken, legs incapacitated. Burt gazed down at her. *Pathetic little creature.*

As he was about to step down to finish her off, the doorbell rang. A neighbor had stopped by — one Burt hadn't yet alienated. Kay let out the loudest scream of her life. Panicked, Burt leaped over her body and fled out the back door.

Neither Jamie nor Kay expressed surprise that Burt's attack on both their families had a similar modus operandi. It didn't draw them together or create a bond. Like the rest of the group, they were just two people with the same shitty experience.

Still, as Jamie hung on the phone with Kay's aunt, her thoughts raced. She tried to think back to the night before. What exactly had Kay said?

I don't know how much longer I can live like this.

She felt sick. *Guilty.* She should have said something sooner. She should have called last night, or insisted Brewster do something at the session.

No, she thought. *That's not what she meant.*

Wasn't it? Everyone in the room had the same thought Jamie did.

Kay wants to end her life.

"Are you still there?" asked Krystal. "I just want to know if Kay said anything?"

Her stomach turned. "I-I don't know."

"Anything?" Krystal pressed. "I just… The police are here. But I don't know what to do. She didn't leave a note… Please — did she say *anything?*"

I don't want to live like a prisoner.

"What happened exactly?" Jamie asked. She refused to believe that Kay — strong, confident, hopeful Kay — would ever harm herself.

"You want to know *what happened?*" Krystal squawked.

"Y-yes," she replied. This all had to be a mistake. If she knew what the situation was, maybe she could prove something else had happened. Like an accident.

Or murder.

Burt did it.

Krystal was speechless. "I…"

"If I had some details, maybe I could see if—"

"Details?" Krystal sobbed. "You really *are* sick. The whole lot of ya. I told her to stay away from you people. I knew dwelling on that awfulness wasn't going to help. *And now look what's happened."*

Jamie stammered, feeling like a brow-beaten teenager all over again. "I-I just w-want to help."

"Well, you're *not,*" Krystal snapped, hanging up.

Jamie laid back down, curling up on her side. She didn't move until the phone rang again hours later.

CHAPTER 14

E mergency meeting, Dr. Brewster's orders. Jamie did not feel like returning to the office, and she really didn't want to see Brewster, but Kay and Henshaw would have wanted the others to stick together, so Jamie decided to go along.

A last request.

Benji was already there, head in his hands as Jamie took her seat. Nick's spot was empty, and Brewster explained that he wouldn't be joining them that evening. Jamie's fingers twitched to send him a text.

Are you okay?

Has anything strange happened?

You're still alive, right?

But the group had a strict no phones rule, so Jamie kept it in her bag. Besides, she couldn't handle another rejection if he chose to ignore her.

"So you've all heard the news," Brewster began. This

time he didn't have his notebook or clipboard. He placed his meaty hands on his thighs and focused on his two patients.

Jamie's skin crawled under his gaze. She looked down at the floor, unable to settle her nerves.

"Karolyn Quigley took her own life on Tuesday night." He removed his glasses and began to polish one of the lenses. "It's always very difficult when a doctor loses a patient and it saddens me that I wasn't able to do more to help Karolyn."

"Kay," Jamie whispered.

"Pardon?"

"Kay!" Benji and Jamie shouted.

"Her name is Kay!" Benji continued. "She hates being called Karolyn, because that sick fuck would whistle that song at her!"

Brewster blinked in surprise, fumbling to put his glasses back on. "What song?"

"'Sweet Caroline'! He'd sing that fucking song! She said he even whistled it when he killed her mom!" Benji buried his head in his hands. Both knees bounced up and down.

"I apologize," said Brewster. "I haven't had much time to get to know everybody here, but I hope you both understand that I'm here to help."

Jamie caught him staring at her again, and she was forced to look away. Even the sight of Benji's twitchy legs was less irritating. "I just want to know what happened."

"We all do," said Brewster. "Even the world's highly regarded psychotherapists are often at a loss as to why their patients choose to end their lives. It's very difficult to process."

She swallowed. "No, I mean... I want to know *how.*"

Brewster frowned and Benji gave her a horrified side-eyed stare. She suddenly felt too hot, too crowded. What a terrible thing to wonder out loud.

"Uh, that's not something I think is appropriate to discuss in this forum," Brewster replied.

"I know and I'm sorry," she said. "But what if it wasn't suicide? What if it was something else?"

"Something else?" Benji openly gawked now. "What the hell, man?"

"It was suicide, I can assure you," Brewster said.

"Did she suffer?" And then she added something childish and definitely not true: "Henshaw would've told us — something, anything."

Brewster sighed. "I want it on the record that I'm against sharing this deeply personal and troubling information with you, but if you refuse to move on from this topic, I will tell you. But I'm warning you that it is upsetting and I'm going to ask that you schedule a personal appointment with me to discuss your feelings on this matter." Jamie gave him a cold stare, as he quickly added, "The both of you."

Benji threw his hands up. "My benefits are maxed the fuck out and now I need *extra* therapy because of shit Jamie says? Jesus Christ." He crossed his arms, pouting. "Fine. Whatever. Sign me up."

Jamie didn't like the way the doc watched her. His tongue poked out between his lips, as he waited for her consent. She didn't want to be alone with him; she didn't even want to be in this group session with him. She was only here for Kay. And because she was here for Kay, she needed to know what happened.

Avoiding Brewster's stare, she nodded. "Fine."

"Okay," he said, rubbing his palms on his pant legs. "Again, this information may be unsettling. If what I'm about to tell you compels you to attempt the same, then I ask that you to call me or the emergency line immediately. Don't make any attempts on your life without reaching out for a lifeline. Understood?"

They both nodded.

Brewster cleared his throat. "So the information I received from Karo— From *Kay's* aunt is that Kay hanged herself in her closet."

Silence fell over the room again. But inside Jamie's head, alarm bells rang, and before she could stop herself, she blurted out: "How does a person in a wheelchair hang themselves in a closet?"

Brewster frowned again as Benji burst out with, *"What the actual fuck, Jamie? Jesus Christ!"*

"It's a valid question!"

"It's a *sick* fucking question!"

"Alright, alright." Brewster motioned for them to calm down. "Let's stop with the yelling. It's only escalating our emotions."

"Damn right I'm escalated!" Benji stabbed a finger at Jamie. "What kinda ableist bullshit is that? She could hang herself if she wanted to."

"Unassisted?" she asked.

Benji slapped his forehead. "Christ, Jamie. Don't you know anything? Haven't you ever seen a prison movie? You don't need a, a, a … whole fuckin' gallows! Just a tight knot and not a lotta slack."

Jamie recoiled. This entire conversation was sick, and she hated herself for bringing it up. At the very least, Benji should be on her side. After all, he witnessed everything she had. Why couldn't he see that Burt had found another way to cheat death?

"I think that's enough for today," Brewster declared.

Benji stormed out, ripping his coat off the rack on his way. Jamie was torn between suffering his wrath in the elevator or lingering under Brewster's intense stare. She couldn't deal with either of them at the moment, so she grabbed her bag and took the stairs.

At home, she dug around in her fridge for something to drink and found a bottle of vodka hiding behind a freezer-burnt bag of stir fry mix. She set it on the counter while searching for a clean glass, and then decided *what the hell* — she planted herself on the couch and drank it straight from the bottle.

Fuming over Benji's ableist comment and burning up under a mountain of shame and guilt, she stared at the balcony door. The same door she had checked the night Henshaw told her that Burt's body was missing. She had problems getting the damn thing to lock, but she hadn't opened it since the end of summer — and now she noticed that the lock had popped open.

She set the bottle down, got up, and went over to the door. On closer inspection, the curtains were all wrong. Wincing, she swatted at the panels.

No one hid behind them. It was safe.

She slid open the door and stepped onto the balcony. No one hid there either.

Peering over the side, she saw nothing unusual, aside from her downstairs neighbor's patio table and chairs pushed into a corner — and a black scuff mark on her railing. That hadn't been there before.

She looked back down. It was possible someone could have climbed up.

Feeling a chill, she was about to go back in when a sudden clatter seized her heart. It came from her bedroom. She froze, straining to hear.

Just when she was about to tell herself that it was nothing, a floorboard creaked. She poked her head inside. A person in a black ski mask stepped out of her room.

They saw each other. She ducked back outside as he charged toward her. She slammed the door shut on his masked face. *Son of a bitch.* She pushed her entire weight against the narrow door handle.

The person, presumably a man much bigger and taller than she was, could have ripped the door open and dragged her back inside. Her scalp flared with the burning memory of Burt grabbing her hair. But all the stranger did was cock his head, studying her.

"Get out!" she shrieked.

He flashed a knife, but before he could attack, a neighbor banged on the paper-thin wall. "Keep it down in there! I'm tryin' to sleep!"

"Help!" she cried. "Help me!"

The stranger wagged his knife at her, like a disapproving finger. *Oh, no you don't.* Then with his leather-gloved hand, he pressed the opened *MISS YOU* card against the glass. *LOVE, DADDY.*

She froze.

He dropped the card and punched the glass where her face was. She jumped back from the door handle. He had the upper hand, but in the moment she flinched, he locked her out and ran away.

CHAPTER 15

The faulty lock wasn't hard to jimmy open. What was hard for Jamie was forcing herself to go back inside the apartment.

Though it appeared the man had left, leaving the card behind, Jamie couldn't be too sure. She picked up her phone and ran back out onto the balcony to call the police.

As she waited, curled up in a corner and watching the door, she thought about calling her mom. But what was the point? Her mom would never answer, not at this time of night.

Instead, a call came into her. *Nick M.*

"Hello?"

"Heyyy," he groaned. He sounded different. Looser. Not himself. "Fuckin' Kay, man."

"Nick? Where are you?"

"Pfft. Out. You didn't call."

"I didn't call?"

"You called me about a … a fuckin' missing body — *but not about Kay?*"

Jamie felt bad, but also confused. How the hell was she supposed to know what to call him about? The last time had been an accident. And when he sloughed her off after the last group meeting, what was she supposed to think?

"I thought we were friends," he mumbled.

She didn't think that they were, nor did she have any clue that's what he thought. "Are you okay?"

"I just had a little. No big deal."

"A little what?" She peered inside her apartment, keeping an eye out in case the man returned, but saw only the vodka sitting on her coffee table. "Are you drunk?"

"A little Jager, a little Ambien, a little tequila… Don't tell my sponsor."

"Your sponsor? Ohhh…" If he honestly believed she was his friend, then she was a terrible one. *How did I not know he had a problem?* "I think you should call Dr. Brewster."

"I shoulda called *Kay*. She needed us. She needed *me.*"

Jamie rubbed her eyes, feeling more tired than ever, but after tonight, she didn't think she would be able to sleep again. "I thought Dr. Brewster would've called you. I didn't know—"

"He called. Fuck that guy. Told me I needed to come to group. No one tells me when to go. I got other shit to deal with."

"I'm sorry," she said. "But it's not your fault."

"It's messed up what happened."

"You didn't know…"

He groaned. "I'm… I'm messed up…"

Someone banged on her apartment door. Jamie clutched the phone to her ear. "Nick? Can you stay on the line? Someone's here and I'm afraid—"

But he had already hung up.

* * *

Jamie answered the door with the bottle of vodka in hand, ready to crack the burglar over the head with it if he returned. But it wasn't the masked man at her door. It was two uniformed police officers with shaved heads; one had a bristly mustache, but otherwise they could have been the same man.

They trampled through her apartment, looking in every nook and cranny for any sign that the man was still there. But he was long gone and hadn't stolen anything, aside from her sense of security.

"Then what would he be doing here?" she asked.

The two officers exchanged a knowing look. "Well," said the shaven cop, "could've been a pervert. We get sickos prowling neighborhoods all the time, looking for opportunities. You didn't leave your door unlocked?"

The other one nodded along. "Or what about an ex-boyfriend, a recent fling?"

Jamie crossed her arms and shook her head.

"You sure? It's pretty common for Tinder hookups to go wrong. If that's what happened here, you can tell us. No shame." The grimace on his face hinted that if that were the situation, she should feel shame.

"Yeah, I'm sure," she said firmly. "But what if this happens again? What if he comes back? He had a knife."

They gave each other that look again. In their secret,

scrunched-up facial language, they shared the same opinion of her. *She's probably crazy.*

"Sorry, miss," said the mustached cop. "We don't have any proof that anyone was here, so there's not much we can do."

Proof? "But I saw him! He was in my room!"

"And we'll keep our eyes peeled, but unless you have any more details, this is about all we can do for now."

"What about me? This is my home."

"Make sure you lock up after yourself. Talk to your landlord about security. Maybe ask other women in the building if they've seen anything suspicious."

"Helpful," she muttered.

The shaven cop's nostrils flared as he exhaled and adjusted his belt. "That's about all I can tell ya." He nodded at the bottle of vodka between them on the coffee table. "And just a suggestion, maybe lay off the alcohol before hanging out on your balcony. That's probably what got ya into trouble in the first place."

As soon as the cops left and she had locked and chained the door behind them, she stormed into her bedroom, ripped a pillow off her bed, and screamed into it.

Fucking fuck! Blame the victim much? Holy shit!

There was a creepy masked man in her home — *in her bedroom* — who had done god knows what, and all they could do was shrug their shoulders and tell her to lay off the bottle.

She hurled the pillow into her open closet, and then wondered — *dear god* — if that's where that son of a bitch had been hiding.

He was waiting to kill me.

CHAPTER 16

O n Saturday, Jamie sat at the back of the chapel, watching Kay's loved ones pay their respects. The service was lovely. One of her cousins sang "Tears In Heaven" to a slideshow of family photos — devoid of the time period in which Burt had been in her life.

The speeches began with a eulogy by her uncle, who opened up the floor to anyone who wanted to say a few words. At one point, there was a line of people down the aisle. When they got to the microphone, they spoke kindly about what a beautiful soul Kay was and how she was back where she belonged, among the stars, among the angels.

Jamie selfishly couldn't help but wonder if the turnout for her own funeral would be half as decent as this. After Burt decimated her relationship with her mom and murdered her father, Jamie split off from her other relatives. And being unable — *unwilling* — to find full-time employment outside her home kept her from meeting new people and making friends.

But she didn't want friends; she wanted to feel safe.

When yet another grief-stricken family member described Kay as a "shining star," Jamie excused herself. She needed to get out. Needed a drink. The flask in her bag sloshed as she stumbled over knees and handbags. She sputtered "excuse me, pardon me" until she glimpsed a familiar face. Across the aisle, Nick watched her. The second their eyes met, he looked away and she tripped, sprawling forward.

Benji caught her from the row behind. "Easy there."

"Thanks," she said, straightening herself out.

"Heading out?"

"Just getting some air." She showed him the flask.

He opened his rumpled suit jacket, flashing a pack of cigarettes. "Mind if I join you?"

"Only if you're sharing."

It was freezing out. Icy wind blew between Jamie's bare legs. She wished she had worn tights under her little black dress, but the dress was already too snug around her hips. It was the only one she owned, and she didn't have the money to buy one for the funeral.

Gonna need one for my own funeral. I should consider it an investment.

She took a gulp from the flask. The liquid burned all the way down to her belly, where it left a warm feeling. She offered a drink to Benji, but he shook his head and stuck out his tongue — *germs.*

"How've you been holding up?" she asked.

He lit a cigarette and took a long drag. "Like shit. You?"

She rubbed her arms, wishing she had grabbed her coat on the way out. "Same," she replied.

"Of all of us, why'd it have to be Kay?" he wondered aloud.

His words stung, even if what he meant was not what Jamie took away from it. It sounded like he would have preferred Jamie laying in the casket instead of Kay. Everybody loved Kay; no one paid a single thought to Jamie, not even her own mother.

As Jamie brought the flask to her lips again, the door banged open behind them. They turned around to see Nick. For once, he had traded his denim jacket for a black blazer and a button-down shirt. The top buttons were undone, making him appear casual and painfully sexy. Jamie looked away.

"Hey," he said, holding out her coat. "Thought you might need this."

"Oh. Thanks."

She slipped it on, taking him in. He didn't look like the man she imagined talking to the other night, grief-stricken, drunk, and—

Scared.

He brushed the hair out of his face, turning away from her. "So what's up?"

Benji answered, a shiver quaking through him. "I was just tellin' Jamie I feel like shit." He flipped up his collar. "You?" Before Nick could answer, Benji changed course. "You know what we need? *Brunch.*"

* * *

They reconvened at a Denny's and settled into a booth. Benji skimmed the menu and immediately ordered coffee and a Lumberjack Slam, tapping his fingers im-patiently on the table as he waited for the others to order.

"You know there's a wake later, right?" Jamie re-minded him.

He shook his head. "I don't need to go. She's not waking up."

"It's a reception," Jamie sighed. "To pay respect?"

Then Benji sighed. "How many times do I have to pay my respect? I loved the poor girl. Isn't that enough?"

Nick raised his mug. "Here's to Kay."

They toasted with their steaming coffees and each powered through a burning sip.

Benji pointed at Jamie and Nick, squeezed into the same bench seat. "You two getting anything?"

Jamie pushed the menu away. "I don't know if I can eat anything right now. I feel sick to my stomach."

Nick quietly stared into his mug, avoiding the question, until Benji pointed directly at him. "Nick? You?"

"No."

"What about the wake? You going?"

"I dunno."

"Don't tell me I'm going solo. Ugh, you guys. Tell me I need to pay my respect and then flake out." He shook his head. "You're no fun."

"Funerals aren't supposed to be fun," Jamie said.

"I know that. I just …. I won't know anybody else there. I'll feel like a creep just standing around, eating all their finger foods and shit." He jerked up suddenly, searching for something, then flopped back down before

sliding out. "Thought I saw my food. I better hit the john before it gets here."

Once he was gone, Jamie became hyper aware of Nick sitting beside her. He played with the handle of his mug, looking everywhere but at her.

She wanted to talk about the other night, but decided he was embarrassed enough, so she tried to think of something else to bring up. She figured he would know she was trying to avoid the elephant in the room, so she was about to make a wisecrack about Benji — anything, even if it was kind of cruel. She just needed to fill the dead air between them.

She opened her mouth. "How about—?"

He turned his head. His blue eyes met hers. "I'm sorry about the other night. It was a really shitty thing for me to do, to lean on you like that, but I didn't know who else to call."

"Oh." She looked down at the table. His hand was there. Her face burned as she admired his long, smooth fingers and his knuckles. She grabbed her mug and stared into the black coffee within.

"Making amends is step nine of my recovery, but I guess I got some more work to do."

"Your recovery?"

He nodded meekly. "AA. Been going for about a year now. Twice a week. Until I fell off the wagon the other night."

"Oh, I'm so—" *Sorry? Is that the right word?* She clamped her mouth shut, trying to think. *Why do I get so tongue-tied around him?* "I didn't know."

He shrugged, his arm rubbing against hers. "It's no big secret. I just don't like to talk about it."

"That's okay." Guilt burned her cheeks as she fretted about the flask in her bag. *Can he smell it on me?* She took a swig of coffee, hoping to cover it up.

"Any word from Henshaw?"

She shook her head. "Nothing. How about you? You get a card yet?"

"Nope. Guess my undead stepdad doesn't care about me." He smirked, hiding his lips behind his mug.

Jamie's face burned. *Is he making fun or ... is he flirting?* She didn't know what to do so she took another sip and replied, "He must *really* love me then, 'cause he broke into my apartment the other night."

"What?" He twisted around. "Someone broke into your place?"

"Yeah, I came home after group and there was a man in my apartment."

"Are you okay?"

"I'm fine," she said, though her throat tightened and tears threatened whenever someone asked if she was okay. It was almost better if no one cared about her enough to make her soften into a puddle. "He didn't take anything, so—"

"What did he want?"

"I don't know." She left out the part about the knife, still not wanting to dwell on the horror of it.

"Goddamn..." Nick gave her a long, hard look. "Someone broke into my place too."

CHAPTER 17

T hursday night after an emergency meeting with his sponsor, Nick didn't notice anything out of place. He lived in the back office of a garage that he was struggling to get up and running. It was a disaster zone — rusted car parts everywhere, oil spills left on the floor, overflowing trash cans.

He bought the place with the money his mom left him in her will, expecting to transform it into a functioning garage. He always loved working with his hands — his mom even bought his first tool set. But his drinking problem and paralyzing fear of fucking up kept him from opening the place. So it served as a glorified space to tinker on cars.

Jamie leaned in, laying a hand on his wrist. The contact sent a charge of electricity throughout her body, and she blushed, waiting for him to frown or shake her off. He didn't. "So what happened?"

"Got home late, was about to go to bed when some asshole jumped me."

He paused when the server returned with Benji's platter of food. Once they were alone again, Jamie leaned in and asked what happened next.

"I chased him out. Don't know how he got in though, but it's not the most secure place. I just figured he was trying to swipe some parts lying around."

"Parts?" She pictured a bookshelf covered in body parts, and at the very end was Burt's head. His eyes flipped open and he grinned. *MISS YOU.*

"Car parts," he said. "Michaels Auto Repair. East Vancouver. Need a tune-up, lemme know."

She squeezed her legs together and tried not to imagine Nick working under her hood. She took another swig, almost finishing her coffee. "Did he take anything?"

"Don't think so."

"So weird," she said. "My guy cornered me on my balcony and then showed me the card again. I wonder if Benji—"

"Wonder if Benji what?" Benji plopped down in the booth. Rubbing his hands together, he ogled his steaming plate of food. He was about to chow down on a piece of bacon when he paused, staring across the table at the others. "You guys didn't take any, did you?"

They shook their heads. Nick slipped his hand out from Jamie's before Benji could see.

"No, seriously. If you even touched the plate, this food is dead to me."

"We didn't touch your food," Nick insisted. Benji grumbled but dropped the subject.

"We were wondering if anyone's broken into your

place, or if you've noticed anyone lurking around?" said Jamie.

"Naw," he said, chewing with his mouth open. "I got a couple of rifles and a shotgun. Nobody's gonna fuck with me. Why?"

"Someone broke into our homes," she said. "We thought maybe the same thing happened to you."

"No way, man."

"It's just odd that three of the four of us received one of those cards and now this break-in thing," said Jamie. "Do you guys think someone broke into Kay's house?"

Benji bit into two pieces of toast. "Pretty sure she would've told us."

Jamie caught Nick's eye. "Not if it happened the night she died."

Nick slid out of the booth, helping Jamie up. He threw a couple of bills on the table and polished off his coffee.

Mouth full, Benji frowned. "What's the deal?"

"We got a wake to go to," Jamie said.

* * *

Kay's house had so many visitors that afternoon that cars were parked all around the block and up the hill. Jamie, Nick, and Benji took separate vehicles, each struggling to find a spot for almost thirty minutes. Jamie cared less about dings and scrapes to her RAV than the other two did about their much nicer rides, so she was the first one to the house.

A sea of people dressed in black flowed through the two-storey house. Jamie slipped in with them, lingering at the door. As she waited for Nick and Benji, a firm hand tagged her elbow.

"Jamie," said Dr. Brewster. His other hand balanced a paper plate filled with finger foods. "I'm surprised to see you. You left the funeral service in such a hurry that I assumed you had an emergency."

"No, I'm fine," she said, pulling her arm away.

"I'm glad to see you."

"Yeah, well… Kay was a good person…"

"You look very nice."

She shrank under his gaze. "Oh. Thanks." *Where are they?*

"I also should remind you about our upcoming session. Just the two of us. You haven't booked it yet, so I wanted to make sure you haven't forgotten."

"I haven't."

"Good, good," he said, placing a heavy hand on her shoulder. His thumb and forefinger swiftly pinched the material of her dress.

Skin crawling, she stared at those two fingers. A scream — a *don't fucking touch me* scream — caught in her throat, but she was too frozen to do anything other than suffer in silence. He kept talking, his voice drowned out by the rush of blood in her ears and the internal cacophony of *don't touch me, don't touch me, don't fucking touch me!*

And then Nick breezed into the house, breaking them apart with a blast of cool, autumn air. Benji was at her side, holding up his fist to bump Dr. Brewster. "Hey, Dr. B. What's up?"

"I was just chatting with Jamie here," he said.

Nick looked him up and down. "You always put your hands on your patients?"

Brewster fumbled for an excuse, and Jamie used the moment to end their interaction. "It's fine," she said. But it wasn't fine. "We were just talking. Look — there's Kay's aunt. Let's go say hi."

Nick shot the shrink a dirty look, following Jamie deeper into the house. "What a creep," he muttered. "If he ever touches you again—"

Jamie rolled her eyes. "What? You'll beat him up? Just forget it. It was nothing," she lied. "Let's just do what we came here to do, okay?"

She looked around, trying to get a feel for the place.

When and how would someone have broken in?

"We should split up," she said. "We'll cover more ground."

Benji clapped his hands. "Alright."

While Nick wandered into the kitchen and Benji squeezed past the grieving guests to investigate all the windows, Jamie stood at the foot of the stairs. The stair lift rested at the top landing.

Kay's last ride, she thought sadly.

Checking over her shoulder, she slipped upstairs and tiptoed down the hall. No other guests lingered on the second level, and it was much quieter. She could think without all the chatter.

At the end of the hall, she found Kay's room. It was the only one where the door was closed.

Sadness crushed her as she entered, looking around at remnants of a life lost. The walls were painted blue with puffy white clouds. All sorts of dangly bracelets and baubles hung off shelves, covered in plush animals. Unicorns and horses mostly.

A painting hung on the wall of horses (again) running

through a sunny, grassy field, breaking through a motivational phrase written in calligraphy. Jamie leaned in to see Kay's tiny, prim signature on the bottom corner.

She covered her mouth. *I had no idea Kay was an artist too.*

No, I'm not an artist. Haven't been for a long time.

She spotted a small framed photo on the desk below. A very young Kay snuggled up in the lap of a smiling blonde woman. Lori Quigley, Kay's mom. She stunning with a one-hundred-watt smile. No wonder Burt targeted her. He always went after beautiful, but vulnerable, women.

Jamie put the photo down and stood there, struggling to concentrate on the task at hand.

Kay told the group that her mom's engagement was a complete surprise. Like Jamie's mom, Lori kept Burt a secret up until she introduced him to Kay.

When his relationship with Lori began to deteriorate, he stalked them through their house, belting out his version of "Sweet Caroline." Then he crippled Kay and slaughtered her mom.

But Jamie doubted, even with so much trauma, that Kay would end her life.

She turned to the closet, opening the sliding door. No handles from which someone could hang a rope.

If the rest of the room had been painted to showcase Kay's bright personality, then the closet was a dead zone.

Chilled, Jamie hugged herself.

And then she heard shoes tapping along the hardwood floor. A board creaked.

Someone's coming.

She pictured Brewster following her, finding her,

barging in.

She spun around, looking for a place to hide. No space under the bed. No coverage under the desk. The flimsy curtains were too short.

The only place left was the closet.

The dead zone.

CHAPTER 18

With the closet door closed, Jamie's mind began playing tricks. Inside was pitch black, but she envisioned monstrous shapes shifting and shadows transforming into palpable mist. The length of the walk-in closet stretched beyond the boundaries of the house, a twisted wonderland calling out to her.

Jamie remained steadfast by the door, where light sneaked through the crack by her feet. Someone entered the room. Jamie backed up, feeling around for another place to hide. But all the clothes had been stripped out. Nothing remained but spirits and bad energy.

What if they didn't clear everything out? What if they left something—

SOMEONE

—behind?

MISS YOU.

She placed her hands over her pounding heart. Its

rhythm beat erratically. She couldn't take a deep enough breath. Her throat constricted and the closet spun around, making her dizzy.

Oh, no, she thought. *Not again.*

In the darkest corner of the closet, two long arms reached out. Cold, hard fingernails scraped through her hair. Jamie covered her mouth, trying not to scream — but she had no breath.

And then the door slid open. Bright light blinded her, vanquishing all ghosts. She stumbled away from an imposing figure filling the doorway. She couldn't pull herself together, spiraling further and further downward.

"Hey, hey, hey."

Suddenly Nick was at her side, grabbing her arm. She kept sliding down, dragging him with her, until they both knelt on the closet floor. "You're having a panic attack," he told her. "You're going to be okay, though."

She bobbed her head, sucking in tiny gasps of air. Tears blurred her eyes, which darted all around at the wire closet shelves, seeing imaginary nooses dangling down like hissing snakes. She swatted them away, but nothing was there.

"Stay with me," he said.

Sinking into his strong, deep voice, she stared into the vast ocean of his gloomy eyes. He looked at her — *really looked at her* — in a way that he never had before. She felt seen by this beautiful human being, and he kneeled on the floor with her, his hands on her shoulders.

"Breathe with me, okay?"

She nodded. In that moment, he could have asked her to dive face first off of the Lions Gate Bridge and she would have done it.

He inhaled. One long, steady breath. Just like over the phone. As she began to get a handle on her own breathing, her cruel brain reminded her of that phone call. *You're weak and that's all he's ever going to think of you.*

He exhaled. Closing her eyes, she focused on the minty scent of his breath. She thought about what he would taste like.

Once she could breathe comfortably again, one corner of his mouth lifted into a half smile.

"That's it," he said. "Feel better?"

She stayed on the floor as he stood up, offering a hand. She pointed to the wire shelves above. "How tall was Kay in her chair?"

"I don't know."

She stretched, trying to imagine looping a noose through. Even if it had been possible, how would the shelves hold Kay's weight? She was at least a hundred and twenty pounds. Could the shelves, even anchored in properly, hold that much? She had an idea.

Jamie stood up and grabbed onto the shelving. She lifted her legs off the ground, dangling. The drywall creaked and the shelving lurched with a groan.

"What're you doing?" Nick asked, jumping to her rescue. He put his arms around her waist and didn't let go until her feet were back on the ground.

"Kay didn't hang herself."

"I thought we were just seeing if someone broke in?"

"We are," she said, heading for the window. She slid it open, feeling around the track. No unusual marks like on her balcony, but when she closed the window again, the lock dangled. She flipped it up and it dropped back down. "Someone tampered with this. Look, it's broken."

"Could've been broken before," he pointed out.

"Maybe…"

"So what're you thinking?"

She peered through the glass. A big oak tree had long ago erupted out of the earth, growing up alongside the house. Two thick branches scraped against the siding, just under the window — strong and thick enough for someone to traverse.

"I'm thinking someone broke in, killed her, and made it look like a suicide."

* * *

Jamie hurried after Nick as he stormed out of the house. She avoided the stares of the other mourners, Kay's Aunt Krystal and Brewster among them. Though she wanted to call out to Nick to stop him, she feared drawing more attention to herself.

Once outside, Nick turned up the collar of his blazer against the cool air and stuffed his hands in his pockets.

"Nick, wait!" she pleaded. "We have to tell someone."

"Tell them *what?*"

"What we found in her room?"

"We didn't find *anything.*"

"The lock—"

"It's circumstantial," he said. "It doesn't mean anything."

"Yes, it does! Someone broke into our homes and Kay's, and *she* got murdered. Maybe we were supposed to be next!" She lowered her voice as they passed two other people clad in black.

"Why would anybody wanna murder us?"

She swallowed. "I think it was Burt."

He turned on her. "When are you gonna drop that? *He's dead.*" His harsh tone was like a slap across the face, stopping her in her tracks. He looked away. "Just drop it, okay?"

"If you don't think it's Burt, then who? Who would want us dead?"

"No one wants us dead. Kay committed suicide. No one broke into Benji's place. And you and me? We're just a coincidence. Nothing else to it."

"But—" She fought to come up with an argument, one that would convince Nick that she wasn't crazy or delusional. But she was at a loss for words. *Maybe I am crazy and delusional.*

"We're blowing this out of proportion," he said, walking away. "It was a mistake to come here."

She watched him leave. As he turned the corner, Benji came up beside her.

"What's his problem?"

"Are you sure no one's broken into your place?" she asked.

"I told ya — there's no fuckin' way."

"Good," she said. She thought about relaying her theory to Benji, but she couldn't deal with his temper right now, not after Nick made her feel so guilty. "Look, I gotta go. See you Tuesday?"

He shrugged. "Got nowhere else to be," he said, as they walked back to their vehicles. "Though I might take Dr. B. up on his offer."

"What offer?"

"You remember. He said he wanted us to book a personal appointment with him. I figured what the hell?"

As they parted ways at her RAV, she wanted to tell him that she thought Brewster was a creep, but again, she did not want to deal with the unpredictability of his response.

So she gave him a nod and said, "Just be careful, okay?"

He grinned. "I'm *always* careful."

CHAPTER 19

Jamie laid in bed, staring at her ceiling. She tried counting all the little popcorn clumps and then sheep, but thinking of sheep made her think of *Silence of the Lambs*, which made her think of the part where Jodie Foster tells the story about her dad killing the lambs, which made her think of Burt pinning the butterflies under the bare lightbulb in the basement.

Whenever he got upset about a mild dispute or some inconsequential family matter, he would hole up in the basement and shut out the world. Just Burt and a few dozen dead butterflies. And he wouldn't return until he perfectly mounted another poor, unfortunate creature.

He was obsessed with perfection and having the *perfect* family. Whatever that meant. Maybe he aspired to be the good-natured patriarch of one of those lame sitcom families, that no matter what trouble befell them, they would hug it out and resolve it in thirty minutes or less.

But Jamie wasn't perfect. She rough-housed and painted wild pictures of sexy demons and *Labyrinth*-style David Bowie. She listened to Judas Priest and Iron Maiden, and cavorted with boys after dark. And she questioned authority at every turn — and Burt despised her for it.

She had long ago figured that was why Burt turned on them. Her mother was pretty docile and went along with whatever he decided. Christine liked having a man take charge. But Burt couldn't control Jamie. He couldn't mold her into the perfect daughter. He couldn't make her call him Daddy.

So he cut his losses.

And after Kay, he targeted families with younger children. No more teenagers.

Benji was the oldest of three rambunctious boys when Burt married into the family. He took a shine to Benji's younger brothers, but when that family didn't work out, Burt moved on to Anna Michaels, taking a chance on a troubled teenaged son.

His gamble didn't pay off. Nick was smart and in-scrutable. Like Jamie, he didn't blindly trust Burt, and soon figured out his game. He was the only one who stopped the son of bitch, but not in time to save his mom.

Jamie, Kay, Benji, and Nick — each one a victim, a survivor. Each testified at the trial. That was how they all met. Dr. Henshaw reunited them to process their shared trauma together.

And that was going just swimmingly — Kay was dead and Henshaw was missing.

Jamie's phone vibrated, stirring her out of her muddled thoughts. She wanted to tell herself that she had been about to fall asleep, but no. She was too buzzed about what she had discovered at Kay's house, and not knowing what to do with that information troubled her.

Circumstantial, Nick had said. Like he had watched a *Law & Order* marathon.

She rolled over to check her phone. Another unknown number. She thought about letting it go to voicemail, in case it was the breather. But Aunt Krystal also had an unknown number. Maybe she was calling about Kay?

"Hello?" she said, holding the phone away from her ear as if a gnarled claw could reach through and rip her face off.

"Ugh…"

She leaned back, remembering the breather. "Hello?" she repeated softly, hand tensing around the phone.

"Jamie," Benji grunted. "Fuck."

She was flooded with relief — but also fear. She sat up. "Benji? What's wrong?"

"Son of a bitch." He coughed, stopping suddenly as if the act were too painful. "Don't… Jamie?"

"I'm here. What's happening?"

"Get… help…" Splashing water distorted his words, but he managed to choke out his final two: *"He's here."*

"Who?" But she already knew. She threw her legs over the side of the bed, scrambling to get dressed. She couldn't see in the dark. Her hand knocked the lamp aside as she groped around for the chain. "Did you call the police?"

Her phone chirped with a new text message. An address.

"Benji? Is this your—?"

The speaker crackled and something clunked against Benji's phone. Had he put it down? She heard murmurs, more splashing. The speaker cracked. Did the phone drop?

"Benji?"

Panic welled in Jamie's throat, constricting her chest. She focused on her breathing. *One... Two... Three... Four...* Not knowing what was happening was killing her.

"Benji?"

She heard dripping. Someone picked up the phone. A breathy voice exhaled into the speaker, then inhaled with an all-too-familiar nose whistle.

"Benji...?"

She wasn't talking to Benji anymore.

"Ba-Ba-Ba-Benji and the Jets can't come to the phone right now. He's been a bad little stepchild. Just like sweet *Kay-ROLINE.*"

"What do you want?"

"A family reunion."

"What?"

"Bring back! Briiing back!" he sang. *"Bring back my family to me, to me!"*

Fingers tingling, she dropped the phone. It tumbled under her bed. She fell to her knees, forced to follow his tinny voice into the darkness. She stretched halfway under, grasping for it as Burt continued singing. Her fingers clawed it back just as the call ended, leaving her with a blank screen.

Oh, shit.

The caller re-sent the address.

Followed by another text.

Miss you, Jelly Bean.

CHAPTER 20

Jamie didn't think. She ran down to the underground parkade. Inside her RAV, she clumsily added Benji's address to her GPS. He was almost an hour away in Surrey. She clenched the steering wheel, again trying to breathe and focus on overcoming the smaller obstacles one at a time.

She wouldn't get there in time, but the police could. She dialed 911 and gave them the address as she pulled out of her parking spot. "My friend just called and something happened. I think he's in danger. Can you send someone to check on him?"

The operator assured her that a patrol car would be on its way.

But that wasn't enough. She called Nick. *Three times.* Each time, her call went straight to voicemail, which she interpreted as him ignoring her. The crazy girl with the wacky conspiracy theories was calling him *again*. Having another panic attack — *again.*

But a more disturbing thought prevailed: *What if Burt got to him too?*

She grit her teeth, narrowly making it through a yellow light at the intersection as she spewed everything she knew into her voicemail message. "Where are you? I think Benji's in trouble. Can you meet me there? The address is…"

She had to lower the phone to see the screen, to switch over to the map app. In the instant that she glanced down, the car ahead of her slammed on its brakes, filling her car with bright, blood-red light. She shrieked, dropping the phone between her legs, as she screeched to a sudden stop.

The car ahead of her rolled along as though it hadn't nearly been bashed into, while the car behind her honked impatiently.

Don't panic.

She picked up her phone and, as much as she hated it, kept driving. She tried Nick one last time and again got his voicemail.

"You can hate me all you want, but I think someone got to Benji. I'm going to check it out."

On the drive to Surrey, she dialed the therapy office's emergency line. She had never before called it, but Henshaw urged the group to enter the number into their phones. "You never know when you might be in a bad place, and if that day comes, you don't want to be scrambling around looking for the scrap of paper it's scribbled on. Trust me."

So Jamie did.

The emergency operator answered and asked for her doctor's name. Henshaw.

"I'm sorry, miss, but Dr. Henshaw is unavailable. Do you know if—?"

"Her sub is Brewster. I don't know his first name."

After a short wait and a few clicks, the operator returned. "I'm sorry — Dr. Brewster is not taking calls this evening. But I can put you through to the doctor on call."

Where is everyone?! she wanted to scream. "It's urgent. One of his patients is in danger. Benji Martin. Can you *please* try to reach him?"

After that, Jamie was on her own. She drove within the speed limit, pushing it whenever she could, but with the Saturday evening traffic, her progress was slow. Once she arrived in Surrey, her heart started thrumming in her throat again.

Benji lived in a narrow, brown townhouse. His black truck parked in the driveway was the only sign that someone was home. No lights were on in the house and no police presence.

Jamie squeezed the RAV in behind the truck and got out, staring up at the foreboding structure.

Where are they?

She positioned her keys between her knuckles and walked up the steps to the door. She raised her free hand to knock, but stopped herself. *What if Burt is still inside?*

She wanted to call 911 again. But it had been an hour already, and if Benji wasn't out here with the cops, giving them grief, then it was too late.

She wasn't equipped to defend herself against Benji's — *undead* — attacker, so she compromised. Knock on the door and run back to the car.

One knock.

The door creaked open.

Oh, no.

The house was pitch black and dead silent.

"Benji?" she squeaked.

Maybe he's sleeping?

And just leaves his door unlocked and barely closed? He faced off against a serial murderer too. He wouldn't be so careless.

She stepped inside. Keeping her back to the wall, she edged around the living room and entered the kitchen. Aside from a constant *drip drip drip* from above, the only sound was the fridge humming. Nothing unusual, other than he had the cleanest counters she had ever seen. Not a single plate or cup remained in the sink and everything smelled like lemon disinfectant.

How could something be wrong if the house was so tidy?

"Benji?" she called. "It's Jamie. Where are you?"

He couldn't be asleep. He had just called her.

She turned toward the stairs leading up, noticing that the patio door was partly open.

She peered back up the long, dark staircase. "Benji?"

One hand gripped the railing. Heavy as lead, her feet clomped upward.

Drip drip drip.

She was getting closer to whatever was making that sound. A leaky faucet? It wasn't her business. She just needed to make sure Benji was okay.

Because if he's okay then that means no one is out to get us. That Burt is really, truly dead. That I never accidentally brought him back to life.

Right?

She scrambled up the rest of the stairs. "Benji? Where are you?" *Tell me you're okay. Tell me you scared him off!*

On the landing, a rifle laid on the floor. A box of ammo had been knocked over. Tiptoeing through the mess, she wondered what was the point of having a damn gun around if he wasn't at least going to scare off his attacker?

I don't know if he's been attacked. He could be perfectly fine, she lied to herself.

She stepped gingerly over the rifle, afraid that if she knocked it, it would discharge. She continued to the first room, a small office. The next was the master bedroom. It was darker than the others because the shades were drawn. She flicked the wall switch, and as the light came on, her fingers wiped away blood, slippery and fresh.

She kept moving, pulled toward the *drip drip drip* sound.

Just a little further and then I'll go outside. Then I'll call the police again. Then I'll stop...

Stop. Don't do this. You don't want to see what's next.

She stood at the entrance to the master bathroom and screamed.

CHAPTER 21

Red and blue lights bounced off every house and window. Pajama-clad neighbors huddled together on the curb, watching the circus of police and paramedics rushing around to complete their investigative work.

Unable to stop shaking, Jamie sat in the back of Dr. Brewster's car. One of the paramedics wrapped her in a silver emergency blanket. Brewster gave her a steaming cup of coffee, though she couldn't bring it to her lips without spilling it, so she held it between her knees and tried not to recall the scene in Benji's bathroom.

One long, freckled arm hung out the side of the tub. *Drip drip drip.* Blood plinked into a sick little puddle on the tile floor.

She didn't call the police. She didn't need to. Her incessant screaming freaked out the neighbors. This time the cops showed up to the scene: Benji slumped in the bathtub. The water was filled up to his chin.

It wasn't water. It was blood. So much blood.

His wrists were slashed. A paramedic wondered aloud to his partner if Benji might have cut the femoral artery in his leg as well.

Jamie didn't know what any of that meant. She was in shock. She had to be dragged from the house.

And then Dr. Brewster showed up. Rumpled and half awake, he ushered her into his car. Her teeth chattered together violently, making it hard to hear any-thing he said. Eventually he wandered off to find a police officer.

Upon his return, he scrounged around for his doctor's bag. Jamie touched her throbbing head. Her fingers were stained with blood. She wiped them on her jeans and was about to explain to Brewster that she didn't need help, just a Tylenol maybe, when he cut her off.

"I'm very sorry, Jamie," he said. "I know you and Benji were close."

She didn't think they were especially close. "No, not exactly."

"Oftentimes, we call a friend or loved one in our final moments to—"

"No." He wasn't listening. Was he the world's worst shrink or what? "Someone broke in and attacked him. He called me. He needed help."

Brewster tipped his head to one side. "Of course, and you did the best you could, but calling the police would have been the best thing to do — for you *and* for Benji."

Jamie frowned, fist clenching around her cup. "I *did* call — no one was here! And I was worried that the killer made him call me."

"Killer?"

"The same person who broke into my place. And Nick's and Kay's."

He gingerly took her cup and placed it on the ground outside his vehicle. "Go on."

"There's no way Kay killed herself. Her closet…" She felt dizzy but pushed ahead. "And Benji wouldn't— Not in a bathtub. Too many germs."

Brewster didn't know any of that. How could he after only just joining their group? He wouldn't have known about Kay's frustrations or Benji's fears. *Benji hates baths. He's afraid of germs.* How well did Brewster really know any of them?

How well did they know *him?*

He just showed up one day and they were supposed to trust him? After everything they had been through?

Jamie wanted out of the car. She tried to put her foot down and step out, but Brewster blocked her. He planted a heavy hand on her shoulder. "Just settle down now, Jamie. Everything's going to be fine."

She massaged her throat, desperate to relax the muscles, to breathe normally. She was losing her voice and on top of that, she wasn't explaining herself very well.

"He's back," she wheezed.

"Who?"

"Burt," she rasped. "This is what he used to do. He'd make it look like a suicide or an accident. He's back and he's coming for us!" She jumped up suddenly, banging the crown of her head against the door frame. The knock sent her back down.

Brewster pushed her onto her back, squeezing in beside her. She tried to get away, but she crawled deeper into his car, his territory.

"Get offa me!" she shrieked.

"Now, now." He reached into his bag.

Where are the police? Emergency lights flashed all around, but no one came to her rescue. She was alone. Trapped. "Help!" she cried, twisting around and smacking the window.

Out of the corner of her eye, she saw a syringe.

"No!"

"Don't squirm," he warned, pressing down on her. "You don't want the needle to break off inside you."

"Don't! Please!"

The beveled tip poked into her arm. She gasped, staring at the needle, sticking out of her.

Brewster licked his lips. Their eyes met. Then she launched at him. He pressed the plunger, flooding her system with god knew what.

"No…"

He withdrew the needle and studied the syringe. "Don't worry. It's only a tranquilizer." He packed up his bag and set it in the front seat. "Glad I had it ready. You never know in situations like this."

When he got out of the backseat, she tried to sit up, but the world tilted from side to side. She grabbed onto the headrest for balance, but when she reached for the door, Brewster blocked her again.

"Oh, no," he said. "I wouldn't recommend getting up for…" He checked his watch. "…at least six to eight hours, give or take."

She groaned, pushing forward. Her fingers prodded his thick belly, and he *laughed*, like she had poked a sadistic Pillsbury Doughboy.

He can't do this... It's illegal. He can't ... drug...

Her muscles failed her, giving in to the chemicals coursing through her system, disconnecting her body from her brain. Before she knew it, Brewster laid her back down. Fog rolled in.

When she forced her eyes open again, the door slammed in her face. The power locks snapped down.

And then she was out.

CHAPTER 22

He's coming! That was Jamie's first thought when she came to. It wasn't like waking up on a lazy Sunday afternoon after indulging in some edibles the night before. It was more like she was forced to swim upward out of a lake of thick slime, but the slime was heavy, weighing down her limbs so that all she could do was float in place.

When she opened her eyes, it was dark. She was curled up on a couch. Her coat was off and her bag was missing.

She stirred, putting a hand to her head, but stopped. She was in Dr. Henshaw's office. Gray light pushed between the closed blinds, making it impossible to tell what time it was. Rain tapped on the glass. The computer monitor on the desk glowed.

A big man in tan, pleated dockers stepped between her and Henshaw's desk. He leaned against it, smiling beatifically.

"How are you feeling, Jamie?" Dr. Brewster asked.

Recoiling, she pressed herself into the back of the couch, scrambling to sit up. Her heavy hands pawed at the cushions helplessly. "Get away from me."

"Everything is alright," he said, interlocking his fingers over his knee. "You're coming out of the tranquilizer nicely. Let's not get worked up again."

"Worked up...?" Dizzy and cloudy, she wanted to lay back down, but more than that, she needed to get out of there and away from him.

"I had to take you someplace safe," he explained. "I couldn't leave you passed out at a crime scene."

Her stomach turned. She leaned over, head between her knees.

"And if the police had seen or heard the way you were carrying on, they might have suspected you were involved in Benji's death. They may have been compelled to arrest you in your mental state."

"What state?" she spat.

"Your *mental* state," he said. "You were panicking. Ranting on about someone coming after you."

"Burt's not dead," she said. "He's coming back to kill us. He was in Benji's house and—"

He cut her off. "I can assure you that's not what happened."

"What then?" she croaked.

"Burt Mengle is dead. He's not your problem anymore."

"His body—"

He raised a finger, shushing her. "His body *will* be found. Simply a clerical error, I'm sure. But it's *you* I'm not so sure about." He scruffed his beard. "I'm glad I got to you before you attempted anything like what Karolyn and Benji did."

"They didn't kill themselves. Burt murdered them! Why won't you listen to me?" A memory resurfaced, hitting her like a frying pan. "You *drugged* me."

"I told you — you were hysterical."

"You son of a—"

"If you can't calm yourself, I'll have you put under forty-eight–hour observation myself."

Forty-eight hours? She had to find Nick. If he was still alive, he didn't have long.

Drawing a breath, she leaned back. "I'm not going to kill myself," she said. "I just want to go home. Where's my car?"

"Your car is where you left it, at Benji's house. But I advise against operating any vehicles in the next twenty-four hours. The sedative I gave you is very powerful."

Rising to her feet, Jamie clung to the couch. A checkerboard pattern flashed behind her eyes, urging her to sit and let the rest of her body catch up. But she couldn't stay. Not here and not with Brewster.

"Where are my keys? My bag?"

"You need to calm down."

She thrust a finger in his face. *"Don't you fucking tell me to calm down! You drugged me! I'm going to sue! I'm going to—"*

Fear fluttered his eyelashes. "No, I administered a tranquilizer. It was for your own good."

"You touched me at Kay's funeral and then you drugged me! *You're a fucking creep!"* He moved over to the door, his large body blocking her way. "Let me go or I'll scream," she threatened.

"No one's going to hear you."

As soon as the words left his mouth, he realized the implication. Sputtering apologies, he scrambled around searching for her bag. "I-I'll find it. Just give me..." His large body blocked the only exit — unless she planned to fling herself out a window. She hoped it wouldn't come to that.

Another suicide, they'd say.

Then she had a sickening thought. Maybe that's what he wanted. Force her to kill herself. Not unlike the way Burt's M.O.

Jamie stood trembling in the middle of the room.

Benji didn't kill himself. Kay didn't kill herself.

And Henshaw isn't missing. She's dead. I just know it. But how? And where?

She thought about her dad dead at the bottom of a ravine after Burt intercepted him on the road.

Where was Henshaw going when she disappeared?

She stared at the desk. There were no signs that Henshaw had ever been there — not a photo of her partner, nor her framed degrees on the wall. Even her handy stack of yellow legal pads was gone.

There's something else I need to tell you, Henshaw had said. *But it can wait until tomorrow.*

What was it?

Jamie quietly opened the desk drawers, looking for a clue. *Where was Henshaw going that night? Who was she meeting?*

She looked up to check that Brewster was still stomping around in the main area, searching for her bag. *Did Brewster make her disappear so he could get close to us?*

She eased herself into the office chair and scanned the computer screen. Just like the physical desktop, the virtual one was immaculate too — there were only three files, and one of them was labeled *Stepchildren Book Draft.*

Jamie squinted. *What the hell?* She clicked on it. *In for a penny, in for a pound.*

The document opened, and at first Jamie didn't know what she was reading. The language was dense — academic-psychology-research-language dense, but then she saw Nick's name. And Benji's, and Kay's. And her own. She scrolled through the preface until the book began.

Interpretations of the Family Man Killer by
His Child Survivors
Dr. A. Henshaw

"Found it!" Brewster rushed into the room, holding the bag out to her. His face fell. "What are you doing?"

She pointed at the screen. "What the fuck is this?"

He adjusted his glasses. "I-I don't know."

"Henshaw was writing a book about us? *What the fuck?*"

He held his hands up in a *don't-yell-I'm-innocent* gesture. "I don't know anything. Really. She was sup-posed to tell you and—"

Jamie stared at the screen, trying to absorb as much of the incriminating book as she could. Choice phrases that included "repressed sexual rage" and "aggressive deviant behavior" had her attention.

But she needed more time and Brewster wasn't going to give her any.

His hand blocked her view. "You shouldn't be reading that. Not without permission."

"Well, she didn't ask *my* permission to be in her fucking book!"

"I think you should go now, Jamie," he said.

"My name is all over it," she growled. "I'm not leaving until I've read every last word."

With a grunt, he yanked the plug out of the monitor. The screen went black, reminding her of Burt ripping her desk lamp's cord out of the wall. "You need to leave."

She laughed bitterly. She needed that book, but Brewster's dark tone unsettled her. What would he be willing to do to get rid of her? Drug her again?

She kept her back to the wall as she edged out of the office. "I'm reporting you — you *and* Henshaw."

He put his hands up, like *he* was the victim. "Jamie, please."

She didn't want to hear it. She grabbed her bag and slammed the door on her way out.

Free from the office, she ran down the stairwell and burst out onto the street. The parking lot was empty except for Brewster's car. She ducked into a nearby coffee shop to summon an Uber to take her back to Benji's house.

By the time she arrived, the sun was coming up, turning the dark sky pink and purple. The house, however, blocked out everything beautiful — a shadow cordoned off by yellow police tape.

A cop car was parked out front and her RAV was where she left it. She didn't see anyone about to stop her, so she got in and drove off.

It wasn't until she was around the corner and heading for home that she took stock of how badly she was shaking.

Phone tucked between her legs, she attempted to call

Nick. She blew through a stop sign. A car blasted its horn. She slammed on the brakes, spinning the wheel to avoid a crash. As the other car zipped around her, its driver flashed her the finger.

Panting, she eased out of the intersection and parked on the street. She rested her head on the steering wheel, ready for the tears to come. But whatever Brewster had given her made her numb. All she really wanted was to lay down and wait for all of this to be over.

She let out a shuddery breath and picked up her phone. She planned to report Brewster, but first she needed to check on Nick. Suicide was going around like it was contagious and she just needed to make sure he hadn't caught it.

And he needed to know about the book.

Her call went straight to voicemail. "Nick? It's Jamie. Call me back right away. It's important."

She couldn't wait another second, so she dialed back. Again, voicemail. "Seriously, call me. I … I think you're in danger?" She smacked her forehead at the sound of her voice curving into a question. *He thinks I'm an idiot. This is why he can't stand me.* "And … and also, Benji's dead."

She stared at her phone, waiting for him to call her back.

He hates me.

Or he's dead.

Either way, she had to find him.

CHAPTER 23

Michaels Auto Repair was situated in a narrow parking lot next to a fitness equipment depot. There were only two parking spots — not exactly convenient if Nick was expecting a lot of business.

Jamie parked in front of the garage bay door. She shut off her engine and looked around. It was quiet. Still early. Not even the fitness place was open. And there didn't appear to be any signs of a man in a ski mask.

She got out and locked her car before wandering closer to the garage. Standing on tiptoes, she peered in through the window of the bay door. The glass was filthy — greasy and smudged. She wiped her sleeve on the glass before realizing the grime was on the inside.

She tapped on the window. "Nick?"

She was already thinking about what she was going to say when he opened the door. Woken up from a deep sleep, scratching his head. Shirtless perhaps?

Oh, uh, sorry to be such a stalker, but I thought you should know Benji killed himself. Maybe? But I think what really happened is someone broke in and killed him. Brewster doesn't believe me. In fact, Brewster thinks I'm too hysterical to know what's going on. Oh, and Henshaw has been writing a book about us.

Just thought you should know.

Because I like you.

And sharing is caring.

She grimaced.

Ugh. Just go inside and don't say anything too stupid.

But there was a more insidious image that haunted her as she walked toward the entrance. She couldn't shake the *drip drip drip* of Benji's blood. His wrists slit from palm to elbow. His glassy eyes. His slumped body. His bathtub filled with bloody water.

Who killed him?

Because there was no goddamn way germophobic Benji would step foot in that tub. He didn't even use that bathroom. There hadn't been a towel on the rack or a bathmat on the floor. There was no toothbrush holder or a single toothbrush, and the bathroom was spotless.

And, Jamie figured, there was no goddamn way Benji would end his life that way either. He was a hothead — he wasn't going to soak in a tub and let all his troubles bleed out. No. He would probably take one of his guns and—

Bang!

Jamie gasped as the door in front of her flew open, crashing against the outer wall. Sleeves rolled up to his elbows, Nick stepped out gripping two trash bags. He looked almost as shocked to see her as she was to see him.

"Jamie? What're you doing here?"

She opened her mouth to reply coolly and casually, and then word-vomited all over him.

* * *

None of what Jamie said made any sense, but Nick invited her inside and offered to make some coffee. He washed his hands in a filthy, paint-splattered sink and led her to an office with a big two-way mirrored window.

Inside, a particle board desk on metal legs was paired with a threadbare desk chair. And aside from a slanting bookshelf and a pale yellow coffee maker, the room was empty and bare.

Nick put in a fresh filter and flipped a switch to begin a fresh brew.

Jamie sat on a lumpy, sunken couch that hinted of Febreze as Nick leaned against his desk with his arms crossed. And boy, did his arms — and shoulders, and chest, and everything — look good in his dark blue shirt.

"Tell me everything," he said, and she did. He only stopped her midway through to pour them each a black coffee.

By the end of her story, he just shook his head. "Damn," he sighed. "And you came all this way to tell me?"

Her cheeks warmed. "I, uh, well… I tried calling… And it wasn't that far, really."

"Yeah, sorry. Can't find my phone." He ran a hand through his thick hair, looking up at her. His forehead creased. "You gotta report this Brewster son of a bitch."

She shook her head. "No, I…"

"He violated your trust."

"And *I* went through Henshaw's files." She paused, catching the slightest twitch of his eyebrow on his otherwise stoic face. "He could accuse me of invading your privacy or say I had something to do with Henshaw's disappearance."

"Why would he say that?"

"Because she was *using* us. She was writing a book about what happened. How we turned out after—"

Nick's jaw clenched as he swallowed. Every taut muscle in his body was a wall just barely holding back his emotions. *"A book?"*

She nodded slowly.

"But … why would she run off and leave us hanging?"

"I don't know."

"Maybe Benji figured out what she was up to? And he lost it and she had to…" His eyes met hers before quickly flickering away again.

She frowned. "You think *Henshaw* broke in? Why? So Benji could almost shoot her and then get out-muscled? That's crazy."

"Well, it's no crazier than someone coming back from the dead," he replied coolly.

Crazy? That stung. She looked down at her fingers, curled tightly around her cup. "No. He said, *'He's here.'* I know he meant Burt."

Nick sucked in a breath, sitting up straighter. "Jamie, I'm sor—"

She cut him off. She didn't want to hear his weak apology. Instead, her claws came out. "It's no *crazier* than not being able to say the man's name," she shot back.

"What?"

"Say his name."

"I'm not—"

"Burt," she spat. "You can't even say it."

As soon as the words left her mouth, she knew it was the wrong thing to say. That name was a trigger for Nick. Not once did he ever utter that single syllable in any of their group sessions.

Running a hand through his hair, Nick did a little spin around the room, and she expected him to whirlwind his way out of there, leaving her behind. Just like at Kay's house.

Before she could apologize or back track, Nick started talking.

"I'm sorry. I don't think you're crazy. Hell, maybe we all are." He crossed his arms. "But he's dead. There's no coming back from that."

"He faked his death before," she said. "That's how he got to Kay and Benji and *you.* I couldn't stop him and he fucked up your lives and it's all my fault."

She hung her head in shame.

The couch sank as Nick sat beside her. She peeked through her fingers before he pulled them away from her face.

"It's not your fault," he said gently. She tried to shake him off, but he held on. His hands slid down her arms until he interlaced his fingers between hers. "I couldn't have done it without you."

"Huh?"

He smiled, and it was the most beautiful, sincere expression she had ever seen on his face. Even his eyes twinkled.

"When I first started to suspect that something was

wrong with the guy, I did some sleuthing online." He chuckled. "The kid who couldn't keep his damn nose clean wanted to play detective. What a joke, eh?"

She didn't think it was a joke. It was what she did.

Nick too had seen through Burt's too-friendly exterior. He was the one who finally stopped him. He did what Jamie couldn't, but lost his mom in the process, just as the others had.

When he made the connection to Burt's secret past life, Nick tried to go to the police, but they turned him away. Who would believe the kid who was always getting into trouble and who had no respect for authority? They sent him home, forcing him to confront Burt by himself.

Burt denied it, tried to say it he had it all wrong, tried to laugh it off. But Nick persisted, and Burt lost it. He grabbed Nick's arm, snapping it like a twig, and threw him down into the basement. Then he waited for Anna to come home.

Nick had passed out from the pain of it all, but when he came to, he used a hammer from Burt's toolbox to bust through one of the windows. He crawled out, fingers digging into chunks of wet grass. With each bump, his broken arm pained him.

He tried each door to get back inside, finding them locked, until he finally smashed his way through a window. The glass cut his brow. Blood seeped into his eyes, blurring his vision.

He was too late to save his mom.

Burt had just finished carving Anna up on the kitchen table. As he turned around, wiping blood off his chin, Nick hurled the hammer. It fell short of his stepfather's smug face. Burt advanced on him. There was a struggle.

He tried to force Nick back into the basement, and Nick slipped. They fell to the floor, rolling around in Anna's blood.

Burt reached for the hammer.

Nick punched him in the knee — the same weakened knee that Jamie had crippled years earlier.

Burt swung the hammer, smacking Nick across the face with the broad side of it. Nick fell. Police sirens wailed, racing closer. He could kill the boy or he could get away, but he couldn't do both. So he dropped the hammer and ran.

He wasn't a foot out the door before Nick tackled him. He held his stepfather in the tightest embrace of his life. He didn't let go until the police pried them apart.

"Wow," Jamie whispered.

"No one seemed to give a shit that this sick fuck was going around killing families," he said. "But *I* cared." He shook his head, chuckling softly to himself. "All because I fell for a girl in a news story. How pathetic is that?"

Jamie studied him carefully.

"This incredibly brave girl went toe to toe with a *psycho killer,*" he continued. "And if she— If *you* hadn't've stabbed him in the knee, I wouldn't have stood a goddamn chance."

"I didn't do enough," she said. "I let him get away and he killed even more people. Your mom…"

He squeezed her fingers between his knuckles until her skin turned white. "You made the pass and I ran the touchdown. You walked so I could run. You crippled the son of a bitch so I could tackle him. We stopped him *together.*"

The heat coming off his body pulled her in. She shifted

until they faced each other.

"You're a hero, Jamie," he said, eyes drifting to her mouth. "I think you're amazing."

She held her breath. *No, I'm not.*

"I was afraid to talk to you, to tell you all that," he said. "I was afraid you'd think I wasn't good enough for you."

As his eyes shyly met hers, she kissed him.

CHAPTER 24

Jamie intended nothing more than a soft peck, but his lips were warm, soft, and inviting, and as he eased back against the couch, she pursued him. Her stomach clenched and heat rose up in her chest, neck, and face. She slid her hands down the length of his firm torso.

Everything happened so fast. She wasn't satisfied with just a kiss. She wanted more. She had waited so long for this moment that she wasn't going to stop until he was completely hers. She cupped his face in her hands and eagerly climbed into his lap.

He drew away with a soft gasp. Then with a surprising intensity, he hungrily returned his mouth to hers, their tongues meeting through parted lips.

She reached under his shirt. Her fingers trailed over his flat, smooth stomach up to his chest, peeling his shirt away from his feverish skin. Enthralled with the contours of his body, she pulled the shirt over his head, ignoring his sudden resistance. She threw the shirt aside, all the while thinking, *He wants me!*

Her impatience, her desperate need, her pulsing lust pushed her to reach down and unbuckle his jeans. He grabbed her wrist.

"Jamie," he said, breaking the kiss.

She didn't stop, didn't *want* to stop. "What's wrong?" she mumbled.

"We shouldn't do this." He eased her back onto her side of the couch. "You're still messed up from whatever Brewster gave you."

Mouth ajar, she tried to think of an argument, but came up empty.

"It wouldn't be right," he added, scratching his head. "You're not thinking clearly, and I don't want to push you into something you don't want to do. I-I don't want to mess this up."

Had fatigue not suddenly hit her like a hammer, she would have dropped back down onto her knees and begged him for it. It had been so long since she had been with a man she wanted this badly. It almost never happened.

And this was *Nick Michaels.* Her beautiful, broken boy. She was here to fix him — with her love, with her body, with whatever he needed from her.

"It's okay. I'm fine," she insisted. She tried to grin, but wasn't feeling it and it showed on her groggy face.

Smiling lazily, he gave her a friendly shoulder punch. Like they were old buddies. "Maybe another time."

What the hell just happened?

He stood up and put his shirt back on. She averted her

eyes, unable to look at him as shame set in. She wanted to storm out and slam a few doors, but had no energy to stand.

"Look, you'd better stay here, get some rest," he said. "You're looking a little … red."

Her cheeks and ears were burning up, and not from the fiery passion that had just about consumed her. She felt like a fool. *Am I the one struggling with sexually re-pressed rage?*

"No, it's…" Her eyelids fluttered, fighting to stay awake. If she could finish her coffee, the caffeine might kick in and then she could get up and go home, where she could wallow in her shame privately. "No, I should leave."

He put a hand on her shoulder, as if she needed to be held down. "It's okay. I sleep here every night. It's not a bad couch. I'll get you a blanket. When you wake up, you'll be good to drive. Trust me."

No sooner did she curl up on her side as Nick spread a blanket over her, she closed her eyes and gave in to sleep.

* * *

When she woke up, crusty-eyed and sore, Jamie had almost forgotten where she was. The blanket slipped off, pooling on the floor and leaving her cold and flustered.

The tranquilizer must have worn off, making every-thing she could remember from the last twenty-four hours terribly sharp. She massaged her temples, groaning.

Nick wasn't in the office. The door was closed. The lights were off. It was night.

Jamie stood up, rolling up the blanket and placing it on

the couch. She peered through the two-way mirror, but only her pale, tired face reflected back.

The shop was completely dark.

Maybe he went home.

This is *his home.*

Swallowing, Jamie went over to the desk. Now was as good a time as any to scurry away and pretend nothing happened between them. They would probably never see each other again — the group therapy disbanded.

But she couldn't just run out on Nick without saying something.

She decided to leave him a note, opening his desk drawer in search of a pen and paper. But all she could find were scattered paper clips, wrinkled papers, a dried-out Sharpie, and a crumpled parking ticket.

And what am I going to say anyway? Sorry for throwing myself at you? Sorry for being so desperate?

The next drawer down was locked. She moved onto the bottom one.

I'll tell him: "It's not you, it's me," and then he'll think it's really his problem and not mine. If she rejected him first, it would hurt a lot less in the long run. Then she could tell herself it was for the best. It had worked for her past relationships.

She didn't find what she was looking for — what she found in the bottom drawer was much worse: Nylon rope, heavy-duty cable ties, and duct tape. She just about shut the drawer — it was none of her business how Nick ran his shop — but something else stopped her.

At the back was a bent greeting card. With shaking hands, she lifted it out. This one wasn't signed, but it was the same one sent to her and the others.

Perhaps Nick received one too and didn't want to frighten the group. Maybe he intended to solve this mystery himself, like he had before.

That would have made all the sense in the world if she didn't also discover in the drawer a rolled-up, black ski mask.

A distraught sound strangled itself in her throat as a disturbing thought came to mind.

Where's the knife?

CHAPTER 25

Somewhere in the garage, a door slammed and the lights came on. Jamie jumped, dropping the mask. She ran for her bag, checking that she still had her keys and phone. She headed for the door, but then paused to look out the two-way mirror.

Nick weaved in between the mess of oil drums, and all sorts of cardboard boxes and tool sets. He carried something in a brown paper bag.

Where's the knife?

She had to get out of there. There was still enough time to slip out the door and run around him. But he was in great shape and would easily be able to catch her.

She would have to play it cool, though playing it cool around Nick had never been one of her strengths. This time it meant life or death.

But first she dropped down under the desk and

retrieved the ski mask. *Evidence.* She stuffed it into her purse and as she scrambled to get up, she banged her head under the desk.

The office door opened. Nick came in.

That was fast.

He knows.

She tried to smile like everything was okay, like it was totally normal for her to be crawling around on the floor. But she left the drawer open. Though he couldn't see it from his vantage point, he would once he came closer.

"What're you doing under there?" he asked, with a wry smile.

"Oh, nothing," she said. "I thought I saw a mouse."

He raised an eyebrow. "You go crawling after mice on dirty floors often?"

She nodded curtly. "I wasn't sure, so I thought I'd get a better look."

"Well, okay…" He took another step closer. His body filled the small space and for once, he was too close. He held up the paper bag, grease soiling the bottom edges. "Hungry?"

Unable to feel anything other than the pressing need to escape, she forced a bright smile and straightened up. "No, I have to go. I forgot I have a project on deadline."

"Sure, okay."

As she attempted to scurry past, his arm blocked the doorway and almost clotheslined her. Her breath caught. He leaned in closely. His heavy-lidded eyes gazed seductively at her, his nose brushed against her hair. But all she could think about was the fillet knife used to slash Benji's wrists.

"Wish you could stay," he said.

"Same," she lied, heartbroken.

"You sure you'll be okay?"

A lump stuck in her throat. "Yeah, bye," she choked out. Then before Nick could grab her or smash her head against the doorframe, she slipped under his arm and walked out as quickly and calmly as she could.

His eyes stayed on her the entire time, and it wasn't until she drove away that she could breathe normally again.

* * *

When the two police officers returned to her apartment, Jamie took note of their names. Officers Barkley and Powell. Again, they stood while writing down everything she said.

They didn't say anything as she spoke, just nodded and listened. Barkley (the mustache) asked questions and Powell (starting to grow a mustache) scribbled.

Jamie perched on the edge of her couch, gripping a throw pillow As the words spilled out of her, she began to question everything that had happened in the last twenty-four hours.

What if I was wrong?

"What happens now?" she asked as Powell flipped his notepad shut and tucked it in his pocket.

"We pay some visits to Mr. Brewster and Mr. Michaels," he said.

"Are you going to arrest them?"

Barkley winced. "Ahhhh... We're just gonna talk to them first."

Powell rubbed his lip stubble. "Did you *see* Nick

Michaels attack your friends?"

"Well, no, but I saw all that suspicious stuff in his garage. Duct tape and rope. And I have this." She pointed to the ski mask on her coffee table, laid out like it was a clue from the Zodiac case. "Do you think he could have taken the body too?"

The cops exchanged an amused look. Were they trying not to laugh at her? "Why do you think that?"

"Maybe to throw people off?" The more she thought about it, the more likely it seemed. Nick had been at the funeral home. He could have come back later and taken Burt's corpse. Or the person who showed up was his accomplice, and that was why Nick rushed them all out. Then maybe he hid it in his garage.

No, I would've smelled it. Death was supposed to have a distinct malodor, or so she had read.

"Okay," sighed Barkley, squatting down on the other side of the coffee table like he was about to talk to a child. "I'm gonna get real with you, Jamie — can I call you Jamie?"

She nodded.

"So here's the thing. We're gonna go talk to these fellas, but if we don't find anything or they don't fess up to whatever you're accusing them of, there isn't much we can do but move it up the chain of command. Your word against theirs."

"He said, she said," Powell interjected.

"So I guess what I'm saying is, unless you've got some cold, hard proof, do you really want to go to all this trouble?"

Her anger flared. *Of course* she wanted to go to the trouble of stopping a murderer and protecting herself —

didn't they want to too? They were supposed to be police officers, for Christ's sake.

But that anger fizzled into disappointment when she remembered something Nick had said.

"Circumstantial," she muttered.

"That's right," said Powell.

Barkley stood up and brushed himself off. "Don't worry. We're gonna look into it, okay?"

She nodded and let them out. Once she locked the door behind them, she leaned against it. She was on her own.

CHAPTER 26

Jamie shoved aside all the paper clutter that had accumulated on her office desk for the past few weeks. She pushed her mouse back and forth until her iMac came to life, reminding her that it had been a while since she had last used it.

Elbow on the desk, she rested her chin in her palm and leaned toward the big glowing screen. Emails from a couple of past clients popped up; she promised to get back to those later. Under the table, her knee bounced nervously. Funny how it wasn't annoying when she did it, but made her want to stab Benji in the knee.

Someone did stab Benji.

She swallowed and opened a browser. Her fingers hovered over the keys. The search bar's cursor blinked three times before she typed in *BURT MENGLE KILLER*.

Every true crime site shot to the top of the search

results. A recent news story about his death in prison — and not his body disappearing — wedged itself in the list. She went through true crime blogs, certain Nick's online "sleuthing" must have taken him down the same path.

One site was horrendous. The blogger had posted crime scene photos from Lori Quigley's bedroom. The room was too messy, too lived in. It wasn't like the Lifetime movie version that played in Jamie's head when Kay used to talk about it. In Kay's version, everything had been picture perfect. Every object was in its place.

In reality, the Quigleys' house had too many canvas bags hanging off door handles, extra blankets stuffed under the beds, rumpled comforters, and clothes sticking out of bureau drawers. But it was a happy, lived-in home.

Jamie went to the next site and stared at a picture of her own face from fifteen years ago. Copied from a yearbook. Young Jamie didn't share the same haunted look that she now possessed.

She scrolled down to find more school photos. Benji, Kay, Nick.

Nick. Her stomach sank. *Why did it have to be Nick?*

Was it possible Nick had learned something that turned him into a killer? Or had Burt's influence on his young, fragile psyche been enough to warp him?

And what if his story about catching Burt was untrue?

She re-read their stories and her own. It was weird reading an internet stranger's interpretation of the events that changed her life. They did not have the same perspective, just reported the facts they could only glean from police reports or tried to romanticize the experience, like it happened in a movie. They tried to position her as a hero just like Nick had.

She wasn't amazing or brave or anything like that. She was nobody. A failure.

Sighing, she glanced at her phone because unlike the others, at least she still had her mom. *Somewhere.* She considered trying her number again. *She's going to have to pick up sometime.* And then she wondered why Nick hadn't tried to call her. She had just sicced the cops on him. Unless they already had him in custody...

They aren't going to talk to him, she told herself. *They're going to forget about it because they don't care.*

They think I'm crazy.

Just like Mom did.

When Jamie expressed how disturbing she thought Burt's hobby was, Christine didn't care. When Jamie caught him muttering threats under his breath, Christine shrugged and said it was how he liked to let off steam.

When Burt dragged her back home after catching her in the park with a boy, Jamie raged at her mother for letting him embarrass her and for manhandling her in that way, and Christine slyly fired back, "You let that boy manhandle you with no complaints." What could Jamie possibly say to that?

And when Burt followed her to and from school every day, Jamie again complained to her mom, asking her to tell him to back off and give her some space. Christine just shook her head and let Burt take over the conversation.

"You'll get your space when you can prove you can be trusted," he said.

But trust is a two-way street. She couldn't trust Burt hunched over a dead insect, inserting sharp pins into its body. She couldn't trust him when he followed her to the park, or when he disappeared abruptly during dinner after her mom complained about the sleazy guy in her office harassing her — only for the sleazy guy to disappear forever.

And she sure as hell didn't trust Burt when she caught him pawing through her diary. It had been a decoy to entrap Burt — because she wasn't stupid enough to leave a book of all her teenage secrets out on her nightstand.

When she caught him, she thundered through the house to her mom. Finally, Christine would have to take action against this blatant invasion of privacy.

But all Christine said was, "Well, you shouldn't leave it out like that for anyone to read." Like it was a cheap gossip rag at the grocery store checkout.

Then one night, before she turned out the light, he invaded her space. He sat down on the edge of her bed, digging around inside his sweater vest pocket for a bottle of pills. The label had been scratched off. He set it on the nightstand, right on top of the fake diary.

"One every night," he said. "I might even recommend two or three for a really deep sleep."

Jamie repressed a shiver. She wanted to crawl under her blankets and bury herself inside but didn't dare inch any closer to the monster on her bed.

He studied the pills. "Your mother takes one every night. But when you wind her up with your obnoxious, vile behavior, I have to give her more. That's why some mornings it's difficult to wake her up. Because she can't. Because I won't let her."

Jamie swallowed.

"Now," he said, "if you keep acting the way you are, she might never wake up. Do you understand?"

She didn't answer, but her wide-eyed attention was enough of an answer for Burt.

"Good." He stood, taking the bottle with him and scooping out a couple of pills. "You might feel better if you start taking one every night too… And if my *pinning* bothers you so much, perhaps you should try it yourself. You might enjoy it."

No fucking way. She glanced at the pills left on the nightstand. She planned to dump them down the toilet the second the door latched behind him.

As if he could read her thoughts, a smile crept across his lips, stretching his mustache. "I have plenty more where that came from." Before he walked out, leaving her door wide open, he patted her on the top of her head and said, "Goodnight, Jelly Bean."

The next day at school, still shaken to her core, she pilfered a screwdriver from shop class. Just slid it up the sleeve of her hoodie. It was the sharpest and smallest tool she could steal without getting caught, and that night, and every night after, she slept with it hidden under her pillow until—

She missed that screwdriver, and over a decade later, as she listened to her neighbors stumble down the hall of the apartment building and slam their doors, every sound making her imagine a shambling zombie Burt coming for her, she wished she still had it.

* * *

By midnight, Jamie's eyes itched as she scrolled through yet another true crime blog. She was pages deep in search results, trying to find a connection between Burt and Nick.

Detective work was hard.

Nick's early years were impossible to find online, but when she tried typing his name and "child" and "early" for the tenth time, the results came up wrong. Instead, she had accidentally typed in Burt's name. Her pinky hovered over the backspace key, when she saw an obituary for Mary Jo Mengle, Burt's wife.

His *first* wife.

Jamie hadn't given much thought to his first family — not since she first made the connection that their murderous patriarch and her sinister stepfather were one and the same. The bastard had simply grown a mustache and changed his last name.

The only past photo she could find then was of the Mengle family of five standing in front of an ancient wood-paneled station wagon parked outside their home — *murder house* — in Burnaby. It was dated one year before Burt killed them. Burt, Mary Jo, Jason, Melissa, and Christopher.

She clicked on a news story from 1995.

At the time, Burt was employed as a teacher. The family struggled to get by on one salary and Mary Jo complained constantly to friends that she needed to find work, but Burt disliked the idea of his wife working outside the home and even more than that, he hated the idea of "some stranger" raising their children at a daycare.

But Mary Jo wasn't happy clipping coupons and watching her degree collect dust. She wanted to teach too, but she met and married Burt in her last year of university, and soon after, she was pregnant. For Burt, that settled it. He kept her in babies until the youngest, Christopher, turned five.

Burt liked to gush at cocktail parties and BBQs that he was the luckiest darn guy in the whole wide world, but Mary Jo was wilting. She loved her children, but being a stay-at-home mom wasn't her thing. She wasn't a good cook, though she tried her best, and she despised cleaning. Burt resented her inability to embrace being a home-maker. When he made snide comments about it, she would rail on him until he was forced to turn tail and retreat into his hobby: preserving perfect creatures.

Dead ones. Ones that never talked back.

Mary Jo's determination to get a job drove Burt up the wall. His former friends and fellow teachers remarked (after the murders, of course) that he was pretty high strung most of the time.

While he was always friendly and smiling, he was not easygoing. In fact, he led the school's enforcement of a dress code after a couple of the young ladies started wearing ripped jeans that showed off the backs of their thighs. He also canceled gym equipment rentals over the lunch hour because the young men were getting too aggressive on the basketball court.

Anything that didn't meet Burt's idea of a hunky-dory 1960s sitcom was under attack.

And then one day, Mary Jo found a job. It was just a little thing — tutoring students every Tuesday and Thursday after school.

No one knows exactly how she broke it to her husband, but that night after the lights went out in the Mengle house, five lives changed forever.

Once Mary Jo had tucked in the children and put herself to bed, Burt went outside and got an axe from the shed. Then he went up to their bedroom. Mary Jo was in bed with a book, her back to the door. She didn't see him coming. He hacked at her repeatedly, leaving marks on the ceiling where the axe swung up high.

The oldest, Jason, heard his mother's screams and knew something was wrong. Wrongly assuming his father would run to her rescue, the eleven-year-old bravely went to his siblings' room and told them to hide. By the time he got to his parents, his mother had been chopped almost in half.

Burt killed him next. Then he hunted down the other two.

He killed Burt Mengle last.

Leaving the axe at the top of the winding staircase, he marched into his bathroom and took a shower. He rinsed off the blood that stained his hands.

Jamie doubted he had any second thoughts during that quiet moment. He was methodical, calculating, and he never looked back. Onward and upward. He was likely plotting how to start over with a new family. An even better one. But first he had to wait until the heat died down. The perfect family being slaughtered by their mild-mannered father was a big deal, and Burt knew it. So he vanished.

While laying low, he met Christine Riley.

CHAPTER 27

The first time she had been on her own, Jamie had also begun her amateur detective work online. She scrolled through most-wanted lists searching for any creep that looked like her stepfather. It wasn't easy — there were a lot of men's photos to scan — but she found him.

Burt Mengle. No mugshot, because he fled after killing his family. Just a close-up, cropped photo. The resolution was poor, but it was clear as day that Burt Valentine and Burt Mengle were one and the same. The bastard didn't even bother to change his first name, though he did for the other families he infiltrated.

When Jamie ran home to show her mom, complete with a printout from the school library, there had not yet been any other Burt personas, nor other stepchildren. Her mother brushed her off immediately. "That isn't the same man, honey. Burt has a mustache."

She turned her attention to the side salad she was preparing for that night's dinner.

"So he grew one." Jamie couldn't believe how quickly her mother cast the evidence aside. "And he has the same fucking name."

"Hey, watch your mouth!" Christine snapped, dropping her salad tongs.

Jamie used the moment to push the printout in her face. Christine barely glanced at it as she ripped it from her hands and stuffed it in the trash.

"Mom — he *killed* people!"

"Don't start."

"But Mom!"

Christine pointed her finger. *"Don't. Start"*

"I can't believe this!" Jamie wailed. "It's not fair!"

"Life's not fair."

"I'm trying to show you something *important* and you just—"

"Your father had a bad day. We need to support him. If you can't do that, then just go to your room."

"He's not my father," she growled.

Coldly, Christine faced the window and started washing the tongs under steaming, hot water. "I don't know where this attitude of yours is coming from, but I don't care for it."

Jamie rolled her eyes, and with the flick of a wrist, Christine snapped her fingers in her daughter's face. "Go to your room."

"Mom…" There was no reasoning with her mother now. The conversation was over. Jamie dragged her feet to the trash can to retrieve the printout.

Her mother intercepted. "Leave it alone."

If only she had grabbed it, or buried it deeper in the can, then fastidious, nosy Burt wouldn't have found it. But that night, after clearing the table, he must have because that was the night everything changed. That was the night she got her scars.

Jamie had gone to bed early, stewing over the argument, while Christine tried staying up with Burt to watch their usual lineup of mundane "must-see" sitcoms. Burt thought *According to Jim* was a riot and blasted it so loudly that Jamie had to jam her pillow against her ears.

But she heard her mother go to bed early, and not long after that, Burt called to her from downstairs.

"I'm tired," she answered. "Can't it wait 'til morning?"

"No. It can't. It must be done now."

Jamie shuffled out of her room to tell them off — *people are trying to sleep around here* — get another good look at his face, because maybe her mother was right and she was wrong. Her imagination was running away on her, or she just despised Burt so much that she wanted him to be a criminal.

Because deep down inside, there was no way her stepdad was a killer. Her life was too boring for that.

Still, she grabbed the screwdriver before going to the door. She peeked outside just as Burt ascended the final step. Hands on her hips, her mother moved toward him. He had a knife.

Jamie cried out.

The knife cut across her mother's chest, but it didn't cut deep because Jamie dove in between them and shoved Burt. "Get off my mom!" she screamed.

"Jamie, no!"

Mouth agape, Burt wobbled. His arms pinwheeled.

Jamie panicked. *Oh, no!* She turned to her mom for support, comfort, protection. Her long, shiny black hair whipped around — and Burt grabbed a fistful of it as he fell backward.

Boom, bang, crack!

Jamie didn't remember the fall or the landing, just the urgency to get the hell out of there. She dragged herself up one of the steps, reaching up for her mom. Christine cowered and then turned her back, disappearing into the master bedroom.

Mom? Something was very wrong. She looked over her shoulder at Burt. He was slumped in the corner, his chin resting on his chest. Then she noticed that he had a death grip on the knife. His eyes shot open, and he grit his teeth, about to strike.

She shrieked, covering her face. His blade cut across her forearm. Twisting around, she scrambled up the stairs. His hand curled around her ankle and he cackled like an evil witch, plunging the knife into her again and again.

Desperately trying to climb away, she saw her screwdriver on the next step. Her fingers curled around the handle, as he hauled her back down. Even on his knees, he towered over her.

"It's time to take your punishment, Jelly Bean," he said. He braced himself on one knee as he attempted to stand.

"No!"

She stabbed the screwdriver into his knee. The tip cracked through the cartilage. Something inside popped. His knee gave out, and he fell toward her. This time she shoved with all her might. He fell down the rest of the stairs and landed with a *thud.*

159

He didn't move.

Oh, shit. I... I killed him.

"Mom?" She pushed herself up, dragging her aching, bleeding body upstairs.

At last, her mother emerged from her room, clutching her phone to her chest. She sobbed. "Burt? Where's Burt?"

What about me? Jamie thought, hurting all over. She cocked her head in his direction, over the railing. Christine whimpered, rushing to see. Jamie staggered to her. "Mom…"

But her mom brushed her aside. "Burt?"

She looked down, then spun back around. *"Where is he?"* she demanded. *"What did you do to him?"*

"I…" Jamie peered over the railing.

The front door was wide open and Burt was gone.

And her relationship with her mother had never been the same.

CHAPTER 28

Monday was the coldest day yet. Winter was on its way. But it could have been a sweltering summer afternoon and Jamie still wouldn't have been able to shake the chill from her bones.

She stood on her balcony overlooking the waking city. She had a blanket wrapped around her shoulders and a steaming cup of coffee in her hand. Her eyes adjusted to looking at real life, having been online all night, unable to sleep.

She was stuck in her amateur investigation. There was no hidden connection between Nick and Burt that she could determine through a few websites, and even if there was, she was too distracted thinking about the Mengle family. Those poor children. And what about their neighbors? Didn't they hear the screaming and crying? Didn't they try to do anything?

Jamie tugged her blanket tighter around her throat. She

returned inside, sitting right back down at the computer, where last she had been scrolling through real estate photos of the murder house. It languished on the market, but that meant Jamie could see it in all its glory from the safety of her apartment.

Her phone rang as she clicked through to the children's rooms yet again. "Hello?" she asked, eyes glued to her monitor.

"This is Officer Powell. Sorry to disturb you so early, but I wanted to call you before I ended my shift."

"Oh?"

"So we've spoken with Dr. Brewster."

Jamie sighed. "Okay…"

"He, uh, didn't deny his actions, but he was adamant that you misinterpreted his intent."

Her blood boiled. "What does that mean?"

"It means our hands are tied right now, but you oughta report him to his professional association, the group he's licensed under. That'll get the ball rolling."

"But I don't know anything about—" she began, voice straining.

"And the other guy…" There was a paper rustling sound on his end. "Michaels. So we went to the address you gave us. He lives out of an auto body shop, correct?"

"Yes, why?"

"No, that's what I thought. Just weird is all. So, yeah, we checked it out, but no one was there. Doesn't even look like anyone's living there."

"Did you see the cards in his desk? The murder kit stuff?" She pressed the phone to her ear. If Nick wasn't there, he could be anywhere.

"No. Place was locked up. We'd need a warrant."

"You didn't get one?" They wouldn't believe her unless they saw those items with their own eyes.

"It's not that simple," he said. "You see—"

Her hand dropped down. The phone dangled at her side. She didn't need to listen to Powell give her the idiot's guide to how warrants work. She ended the call.

I just hung up on a cop.

I'm really on my own now.

Choked up, she wiped at her runny nose and spun back around to her computer. The screensaver disappeared, bringing her back to the real estate website. She mindlessly clicked through the photos, waiting for some big revelation to jump out at her.

It's not a fucking movie. Everybody knows everything there is to know. There are no surprises. I just have to find out why Nick has been killing us.

She was about to close down the browser and all the opened tabs. Except she couldn't take her eyes off the Mengle house. It was a perfectly unassuming, middle-class house. It didn't appear to be tainted by death and evil. Just like her old house in Mary Hill.

And just like the house in Mary Hill, it sat on the market, waiting for someone to overlook its horrible history.

Two houses that were both lived in by the same murderer for sale at the same time? That seemed like a weird coincidence.

But it gave her an idea.

Where is it?

She hurried out of her office and down the hall. Grabbing her keys, she rushed down to the parking garage and to her RAV. She threw open the passenger side door.

By the soft glow of the dome light, she felt around the seat and floor mats.

Where'd it go? Where'd I put it?

The RAV had accumulated all sorts of scattered papers and garbage, and somewhere in the forgotten mess was the one thing she was after.

Between the seat and console, her hand grazed something sticky. Spilled Diet Coke from the other day. *Yuck.* Maybe her next big paycheque could go toward a full car detailing service. Right after she paid up her rent.

Crouching, she leaned in under the seat and felt around. Rocks, grit, and hardened french fries littered the floor mats, but then a card pricked her cuticle.

She snatched it out and scrutinized it under the dome light. The business card for the real estate agent she met at the old house.

In the dim light, she squinted to read the name and number. It matched the real estate website selling the Mengle's house.

Kelly Fiero. "Moving You Places!"

* * *

The next morning, Jamie put on her nicest blazer and blouse combination and made sure to get to Kelly Fiero's office on time. She had made an appointment, but was running late winding toward the downtown office amid blocks and blocks of shiny towers, and then she had to navigate a cavernous underground parkade to find a parking spot.

Feeling a guilty pang in her credit card, she paid for the ridiculous parking fee and then ran around like a chicken with her head cut off when she couldn't orient herself to which building she was looking for.

By the time she got on track, she was five minutes late, red faced and sweating.

The assistant, a pointy-nosed woman in a fitted pencil skirt, led her into a private meeting room and offered to make her a coffee from a fancy Keurig machine in the hallway. Jamie shook her head and waited for Fiero. Her knee bounced under the table, as if Benji's spirit was with her.

But the bespectacled man she had met at the Mary Hill house did not walk through the door. A short woman with a sharp, silver haircut and red-framed glasses breezed into the room in a whirlwind of energy. She wore a slick black pantsuit with colorful heels. Taking a seat, she thrust out a hand. Her watch matched her glasses, and Jamie had no doubt that she had a few more matching sets in her closet at home.

"Ms. Riley? Nice to meet ya. Excited to see a young, single—?" She paused, scrutinizing her. Jamie nodded. She snapped her fingers. "I knew it. Young and single and looking to make her mark in property ownership. Good for you. So let's get down to brass tacks."

From out of nowhere, she pulled out a black leather portfolio. She unzipped it, spreading it out across the conference table. Her phone, pens, business cards, and notepads were neatly tucked inside.

There's a place for everything, Burt used to say. *And everything in its place.*

Jamie shivered. The woman caught it, narrowing a twitchy eye at her. "Cold? I can turn up the thermostat. I run pretty hot myself."

"No, I'm fine."

She slapped her palms on the table. "So tell me what you're in the market for."

This was all happening so fast. The woman exuded power and confidence. If Jamie didn't stop this runaway train, she feared she could be signing her name away to a thirty-year mortgage.

"Um, well, actually…" She swallowed. The woman gripped her pen, ready to write. "I'm looking for Kelly Fiero?"

The woman perked up. "That's me."

"You?"

"Best in the business," she replied, puffing out her chest. "And you're here because you've seen my billboards or my bus shelter ads? Or both?"

"Neither."

"Really? Well, I'm gonna have a talk with that ad agency. Seems I'm not as prolific as I thought. What area are you in now? Maybe that's the ticket."

"I'm actually… I think I've got the wrong person." She plucked the business card from her pocket. "The man who gave this to me is Kelly Fiero."

She shook her head. "Then no offense to you or your 'man,' but he's a big stinkin' liar because that's all my contact info and that's *my* business card. Where did you get this?"

"From a man…"

"Who?" she pressed. Jamie began to stammer. "I can't have someone running around the city, using my name like it's some old hat. Tell me."

"I honestly don't know. I thought he was who I was here to see. I met him at a house in Mary Hill and—"

"I don't sell too many in Mary Hill," she said, standing up. She folded up her portfolio, taking it with her as she marched out of the office.

Jamie twisted around. *Am I supposed to leave now?* She checked her phone; she had only been in the building five minutes.

She was about to put her phone away when she saw a missed call from Dr. Brewster.

"Here." Fiero slapped a folder on the table.

Jamie flinched at the woman's sudden return.

"Jumpy little thing, aren't ya?" With a lick of her finger, Fiero flipped through to a sales sheet. "I've only got one property right now in Mary Hill."

It was Jamie's old house alright.

"Is it still for sale?"

"It's been off the market for a while. Why? You interested?"

"No, well, yeah, but—" She stopped herself and took a breath while Fiero tapped her finger. "I used to live there. Not anymore, not for many years, but I still drive by to see it from time to time. And a couple of weeks ago, I was there and talked to an agent—"

Fiero wagged her finger. "No, no, no. I haven't had anyone working at that house, nor have I had any recent showings. The house is a dud."

"A dud?"

"Can't sell it to save my life." More finger tapping. "I always get stuck with the duds. Thing is, I can't say no. I like a challenge. Someday it'll sell, but right now…"

"Are you sure someone didn't buy it? Maybe there's been a mix up." *Like the body at the funeral home. Just gone.*

Fiero cackled. "Nothing happens under my watch without me knowing about it. Besides, *no one wants it.* It's a little … *'90s chic.* Too much beige, too many carpets. And in this market, no buyer wants to put the effort in. And so it waits."

"And you're okay with that?"

"Obviously not. It's not *ideal* to have a home on the market for so long. But I'll find the right buyer for it eventually, and the lucky person will snap it up. That's the way the cookie crumbles. Over the years, I've been the number one agent buyers can go to for selling any of the city's … undesirables."

"Undesirables?"

She waved her hand dismissively. "Oh, you know. Flooded basements — water damage, that kind of thing. Former crack dens, houses of ill repute, murder houses, and so on." Fiero leaned in. "Oh, but don't worry. The Mary Hill house isn't any of those."

"But you have a house in Burnaby that is," Jamie said. She pulled out her phone and showed a picture of the Mengle house.

Fiero squinted. "Looks familiar." If she knew the house, she had an excellent poker face. "Okay. You're not looking to buy or sell, so what's really going on here?"

"If the man I met is not one of your employees, then I think he may be impersonating you and living in the Mary Hill house."

"And so what does that have to do with the one in Burnaby?"

"I don't know exactly, but I'm the link. Like I said, I used to live in the Mary Hill one. With my stepfather — Burt Mengle. Perhaps you've heard of him?"

"And *he* gave you my card?"

"No, he's dead." *I hope.*

"I'm sorry."

"Have you ever heard of the Family Man Killer? That was him. He died in prison recently, but he used to live in the Burnaby house. So I guess I'm wondering if anyone has been interested in buying it?"

"It comes up from time to time, but no serious offers have come through. You're actually the first person in years to come around asking about it." Fiero rubbed her head and sighed. "Are you going to tell me what all these questions are about or am I going to have to go to the police?"

"I don't know, maybe? I'm sorry — I think..." She couldn't tell this woman what she really thought, what she feared. Because it wasn't possible. Burt wasn't alive. But perhaps someone else was doing his dirty work. Continuing his legacy.

Fiero reached over and patted Jamie's hand. "Look, I don't know what to tell you, but I'm having someone check out the property." She pulled out her phone and scrolled through her contacts. "Jerry? Fiero. I need you to check something for me. We might have a squatter on our hands... Yeah, I know... Just get on it, will ya?" She hung up without saying goodbye.

"Thank you," said Jamie.

"No, thank *you.*" She planted an elbow on the table and leaned into her hand, eyeing Jamie carefully. "So if there isn't anything else — are you looking to buy?"

CHAPTER 29

Jamie was all out of questions for Kelly Fiero, and though the woman's success and intensity overwhelmed her, she was reluctant to leave. The woman exuded the kind of strength and confidence she wished she had.

That she wished her own mother could have imparted.

But like Christine Riley, Fiero was a no-nonsense person, and she wasn't about to linger and chat with some random girl who wasn't interested in purchasing a home. She had business to attend to.

So Jamie drove home. The cloudy darkness and pouring rain weighed on her like a thick, damp blanket. She couldn't get out from under it, and just the sight of her gloomy apartment complex made her want to circle the block and find someplace else to go.

But she had nowhere else, so she drove into the parkade and found her spot.

No sooner did she open her door than someone ran up beside her. "What do you think you're doing?"

She spun around, trying to put distance between herself and the obviously deranged and violent intruder.

It was Dr. Brewster, glasses fogged up and trench coat dripping wet.

"I-I don't understand," she stammered.

"You called the police after *I helped you,*" he said, jowls trembling. "You turned on me!"

"You drugged me!"

"As your psychotherapist!" he shouted, using his intimidating size to force her back against a concrete pillar.

"Just leave me alone." She tried to slip away, afraid to turn her back on him.

He grabbed her. "You're not going anywhere until you *fix this.*"

"Fix what? You're the one—"

She was about to point fingers and shout about the horrible things he had done to her when his face crumpled and he fell to his knees. His hands clasped at his chest. Jamie reached out to steady him, fearing his heart was going to burst, but stepped back. Torn between wanting to help and wanting to flee.

"What's wrong? What's happening?"

"Please," he begged, looking up at her. "You can't. You just can't."

She stared aghast at him. *Are you kidding me?* "I can... I can do whatever the hell I want," she said.

Tears streamed down his red cheeks. Sobbing and shaking, he crawled to her. *"I'm a good doctor! Please!"*

"Good doctors don't *drug* people in the back of their

cars," she replied, emboldened at the sight of a man brought to his knees.

"I screwed up," he said. "I wanted to do the right thing! I-I only wanted to help."

She gazed longingly at the stairwell. No one was coming to her rescue. Not the two cops, not Nick, not even her own damn mother. Just like before, she was on her own.

"Please. I'll do anything you want. I'll talk to the police. I'll tell them it's true, about Burt Mengle. I'll tell them he's alive. Anything you want."

"No one believes me," she said.

He sputtered and pleaded as she left for the stairwell. When she made it to the door, she looked back at the blubbering mess. He was pitiful. The sight of him made her nauseous, but perhaps he could assist her one more time.

"I saw evidence at Nick's place," she said, voice echoing in the concrete chamber. Brewster nodded eagerly. "The police don't believe me. They won't even look around. But you could go and see for yourself. In his desk, there's some stuff I think he might be planning to use…" *To kill me.* "But you could go in."

"You mean break in?" He got to his feet. "I could be arrested."

"You're gonna be arrested either way," she snapped.

He flinched.

"Look, either do it or don't, but if you get caught, just say you're doing a wellness check on Nick."

"It would be a breach of trust."

"Too late for that," she said, turning her back on him. She let the stairwell door slam shut. Inside stank of piss and cigarettes and loneliness. As she was about to ascend, the door flew open. She stopped on the first landing and spun around. Staring up at her with bloodshot eyes was Brewster.

"Fine," he huffed. "I'll do it."

CHAPTER 30

Nick still hadn't called the next day. So either he was pissed off or in hiding. Or he didn't care. Whatever was going on with him, a confrontation was coming.

She felt guilty for siccing Brewster on him, but there was a very real chance Nick was dangerous, and if caught, Brewster would have a better fighting chance against him than she would. He was at least trained to communicate with unstable individuals.

She didn't want to think about what Nick might have done to her if she hadn't escaped from his shop when she did.

So while Brewster handled the Nick situation, Jamie turned her attention back to more pressing matters: time and money. She didn't have enough of either. Rent was due the next day. She hadn't heard back from her mom, nor had she reached out to any past clients to see if they had any work. The Burt situation had distracted her from trying to earn an income. If Burt wasn't out to kill her, then ensuring her homelessness would be his ultimate revenge.

A light rain tapped on her window and heavy clouds darkened her home office. She glanced at her phone for the hundredth time, waiting for Brewster to check in.

He's going to chicken out. He doesn't believe me. He just wants to avoid getting reported.

Pushing that thought aside, she dialed her mom. Voicemail, again.

What would she think about all this?

She tugged on her bangs and sighed as her mom's voice explained how to leave a message. She waited for the beep. Her bones ached under the weight of her slumped, defeated shoulders. "Mom? Where are you? I need you…"

A text came in and she hung up.

Brewster: I'm here, but no one else is.

Jamie: Look around then.

Three dots blinked and then: **What if he's dangerous?**

That was a legit question. She thought Nick was a threat when she ran out on him the other night. *I almost slept with a murderer!*

Ha, he was never going to sleep with me. So full of myself.

She squeezed her eyes shut, trying to stop her own cycle of negativity.

Jamie: You're just looking around.

She put the phone down and tried to send an email. One of her last clients sent a compliment about the project they had worked on, and Jamie figured she could leverage it for more work. Before she could reply, her phone chirped with a new text.

This one was from Nick.

Hey. What're you up to?

She snatched up her phone, but restrained herself from responding immediately. She took a deep breath.

Nothing. Why?

She wasn't going to bring up any of it. She hadn't done anything wrong. *He* could explain himself.

I want to see you again.

Her chest tightened around her pounding heart.

Then came a message from Brewster. **I found a way in. Door was locked, but I reached in through a broken window, was able to unlock it. It's dark in here.**

After a beat, he added: **I don't feel good about this.**

Jamie sighed. Did Brewster need his hand held the entire time? And also, wasn't it odd that Nick was texting her while Brewster snooped around his shop? Unless he was out.

Jamie: Where are you?

Nick: Home.

She texted Brewster back. **Get out of there. Now. He's home.**

Three blinking dots, and then: **No one's here.**

Incredulous, she stared at her screen.

Where's the office? Brewster asked.

Jamie wanted to hurl her phone against the wall. Was that idiot Brewster even at the right location? **Get out!**

Brewster: I found it.

Nick: I wanna see you.

Where are you? she asked Brewster, fingers flying.

But it wasn't Brewster who got her message. She accidentally texted Nick.

Nick: Told you. Home.

Come over.

Brewster: I'm calling the police. This is too much.

Jamie: What's wrong?

Three blinking dots. She shook her phone, willing Brewster to type faster. She imagined his thick fingers fumbling for the right letters. And then the phone rang. Startled by its shrill cry, she almost declined by accident.

"Hello?" she breathed.

"Jamie." Brewster's voice was grim. "This isn't good."

"What's going on? Is Nick there?"

"I told you — no one's here. It's a … it's a mess. I'm calling the police."

"What? Why?" *Are you going to report me? Is that it? You're going to tell them I bullied — blackmailed — you into breaking into someone's workplace, their home? If I'm the criminal, then you can skip merrily away from my accusations?*

"I mentioned the broken window? It gets worse. I found the office. There's blood everywhere. I think there was, uh … some sort of struggle. A fight maybe. I think someone lost."

Jamie bit down on her thumbnail. She didn't want Nick to be hurt. She only wanted him to get help. "Is Nick there? Is he okay?"

"No one's here!"

They listened to each other's breathing for several long seconds, until another text came in. "We need to call the police. This is bad."

"Do you think something happened to Nick or—?"

"I'm calling the police right now."

"Fine," she snarled. "Call them."

She hung up. *Fuck him.* If he wasn't going to help, if he was going to renege on his promise, she would follow through with reporting him.

She read Nick's text.

Something wrong?

Jamie: Why is there blood in the garage?

You saw that, huh?

Jamie: What's going on?

And then nothing. He ghosted. Pacing back and forth, Jamie tried calling him. Each attempt went straight to voicemail. She sent another text.

Jamie: Nick??? Where are you?

Nick can't come to the phone right now.

Jamie froze in the middle of the room. Dizzying panic welled in her chest and throat. Her knees weakened, knocking together as she sank to the floor.

I'm waiting, he texted.

Jamie: Waiting for what?

You.

Jamie: I'm busy.

No, you're not.

Her thumb hesitated. She remembered something.

"I, uh, well... I tried calling..."

"Yeah, sorry. Can't find my phone..."

Did he say he lost it?

More like he lost his mind.

No. It's not Nick. But how sure am I?

Nick: Come here.

Jamie shivered. **I'm calling the cops.**

Better not.

A picture came in. Nick's bloodied and bruised mug filled her screen. His right eye was swollen shut. A violent gash cut across his forehead. A taut wire dug into his throat, just above his Adam's apple.

The sight of him made her entire body clench.

Jamie: Don't hurt him.

Too late for that…

Jamie: What's going on?

No more questions. It's time to come home.

Jamie: No.

Come home right now or I'll gut this bitch… And then I'll find your mom.

Jamie: FUCK YOU!

Try me. And if you even think about calling the cops, I'll kill him right now.

Jamie: Who are you?

You know who. Come to Daddy.

* * *

Jamie couldn't stop shivering as she jumped in the RAV. She could barely get the key into the ignition. She double checked the address, though she knew it off by heart. Everyone remembers their childhood home. The house numbers were burned into her memory.

Whoever had Nick wanted her at the Mary Hill house. *This can't be happening. I have to call the police. No, he'll kill Nick.*

It's not Burt. It can't be Burt.

But it's someone dangerous. And I can't do this on my own.

I'm always on my own.

And now she was going back to where the nightmare was supposed to have ended. But it never did, nor would it ever be over. Burt was with her forever, like a bad tattoo she never wanted in the first place.

It's all her *fault.* Jamie sniveled, banging her head against the steering wheel. *Mom.*

But it *wasn't* her mother's fault. Christine hadn't intended to get knocked up at eighteen and marry her baby's irresponsible father.

Tanner was exciting, but he was shit at supporting and caring for a young family. He was never there, and what Jamie only just realized was that her mom had always been on her own too. She did her best, and unfortunately for her teen daughter, it wasn't good enough.

So Christine gave in to someone kind, a man who treated her like a queen. How could she have known her new beau was a serial liar and family annihilator?

Jamie picked up her phone and called her mother one last time.

"Mom. It's me. I get it now. And I'm sorry. I'm sorry you had to leave." She sniffled, summoning her courage. "But I needed you — I *still* need you — and you fucking left me."

She ended the call and wiped her nose. It was time to go. It was time to face the music.

She texted the address to Brewster.

In case something happens to me.

CHAPTER 31

Save for a flickering porch light and a wood-paneled station wagon parked in the driveway, the Mary Hill house showed no signs of life.

Jamie blocked the other car in before turning off her engine. She waited. Any moment, a large beast could throw open the front door and charge at her like a Texas chainsaw maniac.

The FOR SALE sign rattled in the wind.

She was itching to send a text to Nick — **Are you safe?** — but it wouldn't reach him, even if he was still alive. She had to go in and see for herself.

Her phone rang. *KAROLYN QUIGLEY* appeared on the screen. Her heart lurched.

What kind of sick joke—?

Blinking rapidly, she saw she had misread it. *CHRISTINE RILEY* was the actual name on the screen. "What the hell?"

After all this time, at this life-or-death moment, of course her mother chose to call. Jamie desperately wanted to hear her voice. She wanted to tear into her for abandoning her. But there was no time. She had a new family now, and if she didn't act quickly, she would lose Nick.

She ignored the call.

Before exiting the RAV, she put her phone in her pocket and set her keys between each finger of one hand. It felt awkward, unnatural. She just knew she would drop them the second Burt jumped her.

Not Burt. It's just a man. A stranger. A psycho.

She wished she had brought a knife, or that she still possessed the stolen screwdriver. But when she left the apartment, she hadn't been thinking clearly. And the screwdriver was in an evidence locker far, far away.

As she approached the house, she looked up at the second-floor windows. Someone waved through the dirty glass. Or was it a reflection of the surrounding trees?

Her heart pounded, drowning out the sound of the doorbell.

After a long silence, nothing happened. No one answered or ran up to stab her in the back.

Instead, a text came in, chirping so loudly she fumbled her phone. *Shit!*

What are you waiting for?

Come in.

Licking her lips with a parched tongue, she turned the doorknob. She stepped inside where it was cold and dark. She tripped — forgetting that there was a step up into the living room.

Stupid.

Eyes adjusting to the dark, she considered calling out. The killer already knew where she was. He had the upper hand. *Might as well get this over with.*

But her tightening throat and dry mouth refused to let her speak, and she was left voiceless and uncertain.

He wants me to go to him.

The hardwood floor creaked under foot. She peered into the living room. Nothing — no furniture, no one. Just bare walls and old carpet.

She headed for the kitchen. The heart of the home. She remembered baking Christmas cookies with her mom and setting aside a bunch for her dad so he wouldn't be left out.

Again, no one was there.

The faucet dripped, reminding her of Benji's bathroom. So much blood. She went to the sink and tightened the faucet.

Something clattered and banged overhead. Was it footsteps or the wind? She paused, looking up, waiting for a follow-up sound.

When silence settled over the house, Jamie yanked open the drawers, searching for anything she could use as a weapon. But the place was cleared out. She slammed the final drawer, muttering, "Goddamn it."

Looking for something?

The text was accompanied by a photo of the fillet knife.

I'm in over my head. I shouldn't be here.

She backed toward the door with every intention of returning to the RAV and driving away. Even though he warned her not to, she had to call the police. It was a trap. Nick was already dead. She was next.

As she returned to the door, someone above groaned.

Nick! If she could get to him, then it would be two against one. *I can't leave him. Not when he's so close.*

She adjusted her grip on the keys and took her first step onto the stairs. She took a gulp of air and moved swiftly, heading toward the landing where Burt had fallen years ago.

No, we fell together. He pulled me down with him. He broke my fall.

Another groan from upstairs jolted her back to the present.

Keep moving. Find Nick and get the hell out of here.

But she couldn't stop the onslaught of bad memories, or the phantom sensation of blade hitting bone. By the time she stood on the second floor, she was shivering and weak. Her keys dangled from her hand. She didn't have the strength to attack.

A horrible rotting stench choked her. She pulled the collar of her shirt up over her nose, not wanting to breathe it in. *This is death.*

The source of the foul stench lurked behind one of the closed doors. She retrieved her phone and turned the flashlight back on. A new text had come in.

Looking for something?

Where are you? she replied.

No answer.

But she already knew he waited for her in the master bedroom. Drawing a deep breath, she moved toward it, but stopped at her old room. Someone inside moaned. She threw open the door, eager to delay a boss battle.

Inside, Nick was gagged and tied to the headboard of a stripped-down bed. Eyes bulging, he started thrashing, kicking his boots against the box spring.

On the floor by the closet was a corpse dressed in a fine suit. His unbuttoned blazer revealed several large bloodstains on his white shirt where he had been stabbed multiple times. Careful not to step in his blood, Jamie went to Nick's side.

"I'm gonna get you outta here," she promised, but he was fighting against her and she lost her grip on his bindings. "Hey, easy. Lemme just—"

Something struck her on the back of the head. She sank down, getting closer to the floor than she was to Nick. The thick rug absorbed her fall. Stars — and pain — throbbed behind her eyes. Sprawled out next to the dead man, she read the name tag on his blazer. Jerry Jensen.

"Jerry? Fiero. I need you to check on a property for me. We might have a squatter on our hands..."

Fiero's guy showed up after all.

And someone didn't appreciate the uninvited guest.

Whack! Something hit her again.

Nick shouted, begging her not to pass out, but she couldn't stop it. This time everything went black.

CHAPTER 32

Jamie clung to the warm, fuzzy thought of Nick laying in her bed. His arms enveloped her, and he hummed against her neck, kissing her.

But his mouth felt cold and dead. She tried to squirm away. His icy fingers hooked her flesh, clawing her back to him.

She shook her head so hard that she woke herself up.

She was in the basement, curled up on the cold, hard cement floor.

When she was able to focus, she saw an ugly plaid couch and a worn coffee table. Furniture from her childhood that her mother left behind when they moved. They couldn't be bothered to take it with them when they left.

She moaned, holding her head and wondering what the hell she had been thinking. Her phone and keys were long gone. It was too late to call the police.

A black boot stepped on her wrist, grinding her bones against the floor. "Don't get any ideas."

That voice. That whistling nose. Jamie dared to look up. She blinked, trying to focus on the man in the ski mask. The tall, slim figure that was built exactly the same as the madman who stalked up the stairs to kill her and her mom almost fifteen years ago.

Except this man was clad in black. Burt detested black, once remarking that the color should only be worn at funerals. *Life is for living, kids!* Ironic, considering he was the sole reason she attended so many funerals that year.

"Where's Nick?" she croaked.

"Right where you left him — *Jelly Bean,*" he said. "But don't you know the rule against having *boys* in your room? I'm going to have to punish you."

He giggled, crouching down next to her. His knee knocked against her cheekbone.

"Burt?" she groaned.

"I told you." He peeled off his mask. "Call me Daddy."

It wasn't possible — but there he was. Burt, but somehow thirty years younger, looking about her age now, but making her feel like an insecure, frightened teenager all over again. A wide, humorless smile spread across his boyish face, accentuating his weak chin.

He unhooked a pair of glasses from under his shirt. Modern frames with thick lenses. He was the same man who impersonated Kelly Fiero.

You always miss what you used to have.

"You..." She reached out to poke him, to make sure she wasn't hallucinating. "You're not real."

He smacked her hand away. "I'm more *real* than *you.* I'm an original. You're just a poor imitation."

"Huh?"

He pressed down on her wrist until she cried out. *"Of course* you don't get it. Because Daddy chose poorly. You and your dumb mom. He thought he could create the perfect family. What a load of shit."

It hit her then, staring into his emotionless eyes, that he wasn't Burt. He was the youngest boy in the Mengle family photo, clutching his mother's skirt. Christopher. One of Burt's first victims.

Sympathy pain ached in her heart. He had been just a little boy, maybe five years old. Jamie couldn't imagine how he would have survived the attack. He must have been so strong, so clever to survive, like Benji hiding in a Dumpster or Kay throwing herself down the stairs.

"Christopher?"

"No, don't call me that. I'm the daddy now. It's *my* turn." He touched her face with a gloved hand. "It was you, wasn't it? At the funeral home. I was pretty sure it was you."

"Let me go," she whispered. "Nick too. Please. We didn't do anything. We don't *know* anything."

"But you do," he said, staring. "You saw the book."

"What book?"

"Don't play dumb with me. Henshaw's book. She was gonna tell you all about it. She wanted to bring me into the fold, going on and on about shared trauma and all that psychobabble nonsense."

"I didn't read it, I swear. Just let us go. We don't want any trouble."

He scoffed. "Oh, is this the part where you try to talk me out of our plan? Not gonna work. I know what I have to do. I promised."

"What promise?" she groaned.

"Family is everything. Family is the only thing that matters."

The doorbell rang. Blood rushed to Jamie's head, and she almost couldn't believe what she heard. Someone had come to save them.

"Who could that be?" Christopher wondered. He used her body to push himself up, then punted her in the face. "Don't get up!" he added. "I'll get it!"

Loud stars and lights exploded inside her head, before drowning her in darkness. She swam to the surface, barely holding onto consciousness.

Christopher stomped up the steps. He panted with glee. When he reached the top, he slammed the basement door.

Spitting out blood, Jamie pushed up onto her knees and sucked in a breath. The rotting smell was potent down here — she only just noticed it because she wasn't under threat of death at the moment.

But he'll be back.

Though she had been granted a temporary reprieve, Nick and the person at the door would not be so lucky.

Upstairs, Christopher threw open the front door. Dr. Brewster's voice boomed.

"I'm sorry. Perhaps I have the wrong address. I'm looking for someone…"

Christopher's soft-spoken reply was muffled. Brewster said Jamie's name. A scuffle broke out. Brewster cried, grunted. Something heavy crashed to the ground. Christopher giggled. More grunting. Gurgling sounds, scraping. The door slammed.

Jamie ran to the basement window. Long ago, it had

been her escape route when sneaking out to meet up with boys and hang out with friends. All she had to do was push the old couch closer to the window and climb up. As she used to do, she rammed her shoulder into it, but it wouldn't budge. She climbed onto the back, reaching for the window. It was still too far.

She glanced down to see what blocked her — a body wrapped in clear blue recycling bags. Through the plastic, Dr. Henshaw's expressionless face stared up at her. A fly buzzed around, landing on her nose. Its wings flapped, its feelers rubbed together greedily.

Henshaw didn't blink.

Knees weak, Jamie stumbled off the couch. She gingerly grabbed Henshaw by the ankles. "I'm so sorry," she whispered, dragging her out. "So, so sorry."

She shoved the couch against the wall, scrambling up the back to the window. She flipped the lock off and tugged on the sliding panel. It stuck. *Oh, no...* The previous owners had painted the windowsill. Chips of old paint flaked.

She scratched around the frame. Flakes and paint shards speared under her fingernails. Her blood smeared the glass. With enough cleared away, Jamie gave the window another yank.

The frame creaked and the window opened.

When she had enough room to fit, she crawled through.

Hang on, Nick. I'm coming.

CHAPTER 33

Jamie ran to the front of the house. She shoved the door, but it wouldn't open. A large mass was in the way. She threw all her weight against it. The mass budged and she went sprawling — the only thing to break her fall was Brewster's bleeding corpse.

Skin crawling, she rolled off.

A bright, flickering light caught her attention. The house reeked of smoke and gasoline. In the living room, the carpet was on fire.

Christopher was going to burn the house down.

She had to get Nick out.

A man howled.

Please be alive. Please be alive. Please—

Racing up the stairs, she flew around the landing, almost hurtling into the railing. She barged into her old room, slamming the door against the wall.

Nick's one free leg dangled off the side. Blood soaked

his shirt, and he barely had enough strength to lift his head. His eyelids fluttered as Jamie knelt by his side.

Checking over her shoulder this time, she pried the soggy gag from his mouth and patted his cheek. He was soaked in gas.

"Nick? Nick? Oh my god. We gotta get out of here. Burt's son is—"

"I got him," he croaked.

Her fingers worked at the cable ties that bound his wrists. The hard plastic dug into her skin. Pain flared up in her fingertips and under her nails. Gritting her teeth, she paused to wipe a hand over her eyes. The realization sunk in that she wasn't going to free Nick without a knife or scissors.

"Nick…"

"I got him." His heavy eyelids closed as a slow grin spread across his bloodied and bruised face. He kicked his foot up, his last burst of energy, before dropping it down on the bed. "Nailed him in the kneecap. He's all yours. Touchdown time."

Touchdown time? Was he losing his mind?

They say the brain fires off all kinds of neurons when you die.

He's not going to die. I won't let it happen. But he was fading fast.

"I'll be back," she whispered. "Don't close your eyes, don't fall asleep, okay? Please?"

Without daring a look back, she marched to the master bedroom. Fully aware that she was unarmed and out-matched by Christopher, she eased the door open.

She should have left it closed. She should have run away. The smell of rot and death gagged her. She covered her mouth and fought the urge to throw up. Flies buzzed around, circling a dark lump on the bed.

Her whole body itched to flee, but she couldn't leave Nick — not after what she saw.

Christopher knelt by the bed, hands clasped in prayer. His voice came out raspy and high-pitched. A red jerry can laid by his side. "Oh, Daddy. I'm so sorry. *Don't hate me.*"

He didn't hear her yet, or if he did, he pretended that he didn't know she was in the room.

She inched closer. *I don't want to be here. I don't want to see this.*

Tucked under a coverlet was Burt's dead body.

His head slumped off to one side, swollen tongue poking out. His milky eyes stared at nothing through his old glasses. His hair and mustache had been neatly trimmed back as part of his prison haircut.

In the pale light cutting through the blinds, his skin glowed a sickly pale white, and in the middle of his sunken chest, there was a purple cut where Jamie had stabbed him with the scalpel.

His stomach rippled, releasing a deep groan.

Teetering, Jamie latched onto the door frame. Christopher craned his neck. Their eyes met. Before she could dash away, he was on his feet and limping after her. She was halfway down the hall when he tackled her. Her head struck the floor.

His hands wrapped around her neck, throttling her. "You dirty bitch! You fucking cunt!" Grinding his teeth, he began to weep. "It's all your fault! *All your fault!*"

She thrashed and kicked until she hit his injured knee. He shrieked, rearing back. She rolled aside, but there was no escape. He blocked the stairs. All she could do was return to the master.

She ran. Christopher scrambled after her. "No!" he barked.

Slamming the door in his face, she locked him out.

On the other side, he raged and pounded and wailed, demanding to be let back in.

But he wasn't talking to *her*.

"Daddy!"

Grabbing her throbbing head, Jamie ran in circles. She checked the windows, but it was too far of a drop. The only escape was death.

Behind her, the mattress squeaked.

Every tiny hair on the back of Jamie's neck stood at attention.

And then a man moaned.

It wasn't Christopher — he was stuck on the other side of the door, and it was only a matter of time before he broke in.

Hackles raised, she slowly turned around.

Burt sat up on the edge of the bed. He looked every inch an old, rigid senior waking up roughly from a nap. He adjusted his glasses. *Lemme get a good look atcha.*

Jamie's muscles turned to jelly.

Jelly Bean... No, no, no, no—

He stood up with a groan. Wobbling on his feet, he lurched forward. Arms outstretched, he put his next foot forward. And again, and again. He staggered toward Jamie like the villain in an old mummy flick.

In one of his grasping hands, he held the fillet knife.

Come to Daddy.

Whimpering, she turned back to the window and tried

to pry it open. A meaty hand clasped her shoulder, jerking her around. She screamed, throwing a fist into his chest. He hurled her to the floor and dove on top of her.

"No!"

She tried to shove him off, but he was bigger and stronger. As she squirmed and fought, he pressed down harder. He drove the knife into her shoulder. Her arm went limp and she cried out.

He grinned, tongue slithering out to lick his lips.

He ripped out the knife, tracing the tip across her chest to her opposite arm. He overpowered her. He spread her wide open — he was pinning her down. Like a butterfly.

Oh, no! Oh, god—

His body weight suffocated her. His skin felt like ice. Black fluid oozed from the scalpel wound in his chest, dripping onto Jamie.

She strained to look away — but that wound was the answer. It was what started all of this. She had opened Pandora's box. Her hate and anger brought him back to life. It was up to her to stop him. The only way out was *through…*

Gritting her teeth, she pressed two fingers against the slit. His flesh gave way, soft and spongy. *Welcoming.* It slurped her up. She squeezed her eyes shut and pushed. Once she was knuckles-deep, her entire fist slid inside his chest cavity, reaching through a rib cage built like a jigsaw puzzle. The interior of his body was strange. Wet gore sucked her in until she was wrist deep.

Her knuckles brushed a chunk of ice. So solid and cold, it gave her frostbite. His heart. Fighting the instinct to withdraw, she wrapped her hand around it and squeezed.

Burt grunted and chortled. His leering grimace was so close to her face. His mustache scraped her nose — so close he could bite it off.

The icy organ cracked. Too-hot liquid rushed out of his body, bleeding down her hand and wrist. She let go, retreating. His body sagged, toppling aside. With a final wheeze, he dropped dead.

At last.

Before Jamie could jump to her feet, before she could wrap her head around the magnitude of what just happened, the door burst open and Christopher stormed in.

Upon seeing his father's mutilated body slumped next to Jamie, caught literally red-handed, he tore across the room with a screech.

CHAPTER 34

Christopher dragged Burt's lifeless body away from Jamie. He held him, begging, *"Don't leave me!"* But Burt didn't budge. He just slid limply out of his son's arms.

When Jamie attempted to get up, he grabbed her. *"You killed him,"* he growled, wrenching the blade in her shoulder until she screamed.

"Stop!"

"He was *my* daddy, and you stole him!" He spat in her face. *"You took him from me!"*

"He was a monster!" she cried.

"He was my family!"

"He *killed* your family!"

Christopher roared, slashing at her wrists as she tried to defend herself.

Blood gurgled up through her broken flesh, soaking her clothes and the bed. She wept, unable to buck him off or catch her breath.

"I'm a good boy — Daddy says so," he sniveled, cutting across one of her old scars. "The others were bad. Disappointments. They didn't deserve him. They didn't deserve his love."

Satisfied with his destruction, he kicked her aside.

Jamie gasped. Shock shuddered through her body. She was bleeding out fast.

Christopher vanished for a moment. When he returned, he had the jerry can. Gasoline fumes, black smoke, and death stifled the air.

"When the police get here, they'll see," he rambled. "It'll all make sense. Crazy Jamie… Lost her mind 'cause she couldn't have her Daddy… couldn't share him with the others. Henshaw's book will tell all about it. I'll make sure. And everyone will know… If Crazy Jamie couldn't have Daddy, no one else could either."

Jamie closed her eyes. The only thing that stopped her from fading into a deep, unwakeable sleep was Nick's hollering. The sound didn't seem to bother Christopher, who poured a trail of gas while whistling "My Bonnie Lies over the Ocean." Every few moments, he choked on the thickening smoke, but picked up again as jauntily as he began.

Jamie turned her head. Eyelids heavy, she caught the glint of the fillet knife. She was as good as dead to Christopher — what use was the knife to him now?

She hugged her bleeding arms to her stomach. She had no time to wait. Shakily, she took the knife. Hiding it close to her body, she kept still until Christopher trailed out of the room and down the hall.

He clomped into her old room and Nick shouted.

Her grip weakening, Jamie pushed herself up and stumbled after him. Inside the room, Christopher loomed over Nick, shaking out every last drop. His whole body rippled, and Jamie couldn't tell if he was laughing or sobbing.

Nick jerked and twisted, unable to stop the assault.

As silently as a shadow, Jamie crept up behind Christopher. She was about to stick him with the knife when he spun around. He flicked open a cheap lighter. The flame stopped her. Christopher giggled, shadows dancing on his face.

"Don't," she breathed.

"Too late." He tipped his hand. "It's time for your punishment."

"He didn't love you!" The words broke out of her mouth, freezing the stupid grin on his shiny face. His hand locked around the lighter.

It was a horrible thing to say. He had lost his family too. Burt took everyone and everything away from his son.

But that didn't entitle Christopher to continue his terrible legacy.

"I'm his son!" he snapped.

"Yeah, well," she said. "He chose me — but he was *stuck* with you."

Growling, he charged at her. The lighter slipped out his hand, dropping to the floor unlit. Jamie cowered backward, hitting the doorframe. Christopher was in her face, jaws snapping.

Warm blood washed over her. They both looked down at the knife in her hands — and in his gut.

He sucked in one last horrid breath, sinking to his

knees. He fell onto his side, one arm reaching out into the hall, leaving the knife in Jamie's hands.

Jamie ran to Nick and sawed at the cable ties until he was free. He sat up, rubbing the circulation back into his wrists and, unable to speak, she tugged on him, urging him to move. He pointed to his ankle. One more tie. She sawed that one too and then he was free.

"Come on," she coughed, helping him up. His body weighed heavily on her shoulder, making her dizzy.

They turned to the door. Hunched over, Christopher hobbled down the hallway, back to the master bedroom. He glanced back.

"Come on!" Nick yelled at him. "Don't be stupid!"

Tears in his eyes, Christopher giggled. He closed the door on them. Nick burst forward to stop him, to drag his ass out, make him face up to his crimes, but Jamie was fading fast. She wasn't going to make it. With the last of her strength, she tugged on Nick's arm.

Please...

Nick pulled her close and hauled her down the stairs. They stumbled down, down, down. Lightheaded and starved for oxygen, Jamie imagined Christopher and Burt chomping at her heels.

On the main floor, flames licked the walls and tore up the curtains. The raging fire ravaged everything in its path. Jamie couldn't see through the smoke, her eyelids too heavy.

They tripped over Brewster's body. Nick pushed him aside and threw open the door.

And then a familiar tune tickled her ears, making her twitch. From above, a voice sang out. *"Briiiing back! Briiiing back! Briiiing back my Daddy to me! To me!"*

Above, Christopher's singing devolved into heaving sobs until the smoke overtook him too, and all he could do was hack and cough.

For one crazy moment, Jamie was certain she heard Burt. She wanted to run back upstairs to be sure she killed him, but she was too weak to do anything other than let Nick carry her outside, where they collapsed on the dewy front lawn, gasping for air.

Flat out on her back, she pointed to the house. Though every inch of her body hurt, her heart ached at the sight of the fire devouring her childhood home.

Nick got back on his feet, rushing back into the house. He returned moments later, dragging out Brewster's corpse.

Jamie tried to sit up. "Henshaw," she croaked. "She's in the basement. She's—" A coughing fit cut her off.

Nick flopped down beside her, holding his stomach. "Jamie…"

She reached out to see what damage Christopher had done to him — when she saw that her arms had been shredded open. Her stomach dropped. "Nick…?"

His grim, pained face came close to hers as he gently laid her back down. "It's over," he promised. "Just breathe."

She nodded, tears blurring her vision and clogging her throat. She stared up at the sky, listening to Nick guide her. *Just breathe, count the stars.* But she couldn't see any stars through the dense smoke. Tears spilled down the sides of her face.

Don't think about how bad this is. Don't think about dying.

Don't think about Mom.

She stared up at the master bedroom window. She saw her mother. She closed her eyes. When she opened them, the impossible specter above remained — only it hadn't been her mother.

The figure waved. His mustache twitched into a smile. His whistling nose and heavy breathing were so loud inside her mind that she couldn't hear anything else, not even the fire. Not even the house collapsing.

He didn't need a phone line to get inside her head. He had always been there. He would always be there.

Unable to fight any longer, she shut her eyes. Her body went limp. Sirens echoed in the distance. A fire rescue team was on the way. She smiled. Maybe they would see what she saw. Maybe they would see that she wasn't crazy after all.

Nick touched her face. "Jamie? Jamie? Oh, fuck. Jamie? Stay with me. It's going to be okay. *Jamie—?*"

The last thing she heard before blacking out was an agonizing howl from deep inside the house. A desperate, sick man screamed for his daddy as hellfire consumed them both.

CHAPTER 35

By the time she was allowed to leave the hospital, Jamie was stitched up and her pain was under control. But somehow, she felt worse.

Though her rent was still due, her mother thankfully came through at the eleventh hour. Feeling guilty for not rushing to her daughter's side, she transferred enough funds to cover her rent for three months.

But Jamie still had no job prospects and no idea if Nick was okay. No one could give her any information, so she worried about him and racked her brain for some way to call him. The fire toasted her phone and she couldn't remember his number.

Then on the morning she was discharged, he appeared in her hospital room, leaning in the doorway.

"Need a ride?" he asked, spinning his keys around his finger.

So surprised and elated to see him in the flesh, she

almost broke out across the room to jump into his arms. But she held back, body buzzing with electricity, ashamed for ever thinking he would harm anyone.

"Yes!" she said eagerly.

"You up for a coffee first?" he asked. "I think we should talk."

Their last coffee ended terribly, but she agreed.

Before they could leave, a police detective in a coat damp from the rain arrived to confirm some final details. Butting in on their plans, Detective Turner led them down to the hospital cafeteria where they ordered stale coffee from a machine.

When the three settled at a wobbly table, a chill ran up Jamie's back. She feared the detective was going to tell them that Christopher got away, limping off into the forest to hide until he could finish what he started or find his next victim. Like father, like son.

Detective Turner began by asking how much they knew about Christopher Mengle.

"Nothing," said Nick.

"I thought he was supposed to be dead," said Jamie.

"Five-year-old Christopher managed to survive his father's massacre," Turner explained. "One of our psychologists theorizes that the boy's love for his father, combined with the trauma he endured that night, led to Christopher being unable to reconcile his father's violent act. We don't know why or how, but he managed to survive. Everything was kept under wraps to protect the child and he was put into foster care. That's where we lost track of him."

"Good to know the system works," Nick said coldly.

"Now it's my job to figure out why he went after you

two, as well as Benji Martin and Karolyn Quigley. I have my theories, but if you know anything that could help…?"

Jamie and Nick exchanged a look. "I dunno. He told me we were disappointments and didn't deserve his dad's love." She looked down, unable to say what she suspected — that Christopher was finishing his father's business. "How did he get the body?"

"Seems Christopher paid several visits to his father in prison," said the detective. "We suspect father and son reunited and had a few heart-to-heart talks about the future. In one recorded conversation, he promised to help Mengle get out."

"And the cops didn't jump on him right then and there?" Jamie asked.

"Well, no. The context of the conversation was about parole possibilities, but it's likely they were speaking in code."

Because there's no way that man was getting paroled.

"Bastard didn't need any help — he croaked," said Nick. "That was his get-out-of-jail-free card."

"Are they sure he was dead?" Jamie asked. "It wasn't the first time he faked everyone out."

"The medical examiner checked him out," said Turner. "Natural causes."

"Lucky bastard," Nick muttered into his bitter coffee. "Peaceful death for a violent life."

Jamie wished they could have seen his truly violent end: her wrist-deep in Burt's sagging, foul chest. She shuddered, catching Nick's eye.

"Typically when a person expires in prison, the province disposes of the remains, unless someone is designated as the next of kin. In Mengle's case, that was

Christopher, and he requested the body be taken to a funeral home for a proper burial."

"But why did he steal it?" Jamie laced her fingers around her cup, the temperature warming her freezing hands.

"We believe it was part of the plan," said the detective. "Easier to steal from a funeral home than a federal prison. We also found out that he paid off an employee at the home to provide him access."

Nick shook his head, saying nothing.

Jamie remembered the night they broke in. Two embalming rooms. The unlocked door that led to Burt. Car headlights flashed. The front door opened. Nick rushed in to warn them that someone was coming. Her hand plunged the scalpel into Burt's chest—

I didn't bring him back to life — it was Christopher who resurrected his legacy.

"But you're sure he's really dead?" she asked. "Christopher, I mean?" *And Burt. Always Burt.*

Turner nodded. "He's dead. The stab wound to his stomach did a number on him, but the M.E.'s report says smoke inhalation did him in first. The gasoline on his clothes and the close proximity to the fire didn't make his last moments very peaceful."

Fuck peaceful, thought Jamie. Henshaw didn't get any peace, nor did her family during the time she was missing. "What about Dr. Henshaw's book? She was writing about us."

"Did you read it?"

No, but— "I saw enough."

"It wasn't finished. Probably won't ever be. And to put your minds at ease, the book was about Christopher. I think she intended to write about how she came to be your group's therapist, but then she started treating Christopher. He revealed his true identity and they built up a rapport. We're still trying to determine a timeline, but we think he was using her to get close to your group."

"Is that it?" Nick asked. "Can we go now?"

Turner finished his coffee, crumpling up the cup and tossing it into a nearby trash can.

"Just one more thing... I reviewed some security footage from the night Burt Mengle's body was stolen." He reached into his coat and pulled out three sheets of paper, folded into quarters. He spread them out on the table.

Trying not to grimace, Jamie looked over each piece of paper. Each page was a poor resolution screen capture of four people in a dark hallway: Nick's terribly blurred shape as he pushed Kay to the door, Benji clear as day looking up at the camera, and Jamie turned around to see who was behind them.

"Looks like your friends were there that night," Turner said. "But I can't seem to make out the other two. Anyone look familiar?"

"Could be anybody," said Nick.

Jamie swallowed and pushed the papers back to the detective. "I can't make out a thing."

Chewing the inside of his cheek, Turner folded up the papers and returned them to his coat pocket. "No, me neither."

"Did they cause any of this to happen?" Jamie asked.

"I don't suspect so," he said. "But they were damn lucky to get away when they did. Who knows how Christopher might have reacted — seeing at that moment the very people he blamed for stealing his father away."

Jamie nodded solemnly, thinking about all the lives his bastard father stole. It wasn't fair, but what in life was?

Turner stood up and Jamie and Nick followed suit. He shook their hands and wished them well, promising to be in touch as needed. They thanked him and parted ways.

Jamie and Nick didn't speak until they were in his Mustang about to leave the hospital.

"You think Christopher would've done something?" he asked.

"At the funeral home?"

"Yeah," he said, rubbing his chin. "He had us dead to rights."

Jamie shook her head. "No. He's one person."

"One person who killed five people."

"But we were four strong."

"Strong? Scared shitless is more like it."

"Maybe, but we had each other's backs, even if it didn't feel like it. Strange as it sounds, the four of us were kind of like a family. We shared the same experience, the same trauma. If he had joined our group, maybe we could have helped him. But instead, he was just like his dad. Just like Burt. Dismantling the family unit one by one until we were vulnerable enough to destroy."

Nick rubbed his chin. "Son of a bitch."

They drove in silence to her apartment. Nick only spoke up to ask for directions. She kept thinking about that night, crushing Burt's heart, and then she couldn't hold it in any longer.

"I saw him," she said, stroking her frostbitten fingers. "In the window. Maybe I was seeing things or I really am crazy, but goddamn it, he was *there.*"

If Nick didn't believe her, if he thought she was crazy, then they never had to see each other again.

Instead of shutting her down or telling her she was suffering from smoke inhalation, Nick grabbed her hands and held them against his chest. The bandages around her wrists chafed, but his pounding heart grounded her.

When he spoke, she knew she wasn't dreaming or hallucinating.

"I saw him too."

AFTER

Two days before Christmas, chaos descended on Vancouver International Airport. People parked crookedly and illegally near the doors to the departures entrance, racing out of their vehicles to haul too much luggage onto their pre-Christmas flights. Tires spit slush and ice as hurried drivers zipped away.

One lucky driver found a spot just outside one of the doors.

Jamie put the RAV4 in park as Nick climbed out. He swiftly opened the rear door and hefted her suitcase from the backseat before she even set foot on the ground. She was about to admonish him for lifting too much weight while he was still recovering, but he shot her a look that said, *Relax, I'm fine.*

She surrendered her keys.

"Take care of her, okay?" she said, feeling anxious about leaving her only mode of transportation with someone else.

He looped the ring over his finger, cradling the keys in his palm. "Don't worry. I'll have her all tuned up for ya when you get back. Have a good time in… Where in Florida again?"

"Fort Myers." She adjusted the carry-on bag on her shoulder. The action set off a flare of pain, but she gritted her teeth through it. "And, uh, thanks for driving me. I know you're busy getting the shop up and running."

"It's the least I could do, considering you saved my life," he said, flipping his hair off his face.

She blushed, thinking about how badly she wanted to touch his hair, brush it out of his face and away from his scarred eyebrow. Biting her lip, she reached up and—

"Have a good flight," he said.

She bit down on a squeak and dropped her hand. "Thanks, I will." *Stupid. I don't control the plane. The flight will be what it's going to be.* And it was going to be pretty lousy with an overnight connection in Toronto.

But that wasn't the only thing that made her feel stupid. Though they had met up for coffee several times, nothing romantic had transpired between them. There had been a few awkward pauses and longing looks, but nothing else, and besides, it took weeks for Jamie's arms to heal and begin to feel somewhat normal enough to hug someone.

It's just not meant to be.

"And Merry Christmas," he added.

"I don't know how *merry* it's going to be," she said. "My mom and I have a lot of stuff to work out."

"It'll be fine," he said. "She'll be happy to see you."

"Yeah, maybe. I'm just … worried, you know?"

Even if her mother drove her nuts most of the time and had problems of her own, they needed to make things right. Jamie accepted that they would never be as close as they were before Burt came between them, but they had to try to mend their relationship.

If Burt was right about one thing, it was that family was important.

"I know."

Nick's gazed drifted off. He didn't have his mom around to get into holiday-fueled arguments with. He was going to be all by himself, probably microwaving a TV dinner.

"Are you going to be alright?" she asked.

He shrugged, a typical tough guy gesture. "I can manage."

"Are you sure?"

"I'll be fine. I've spent a lot of holidays without anyone looking after me. Besides, you still have your mom and she wants to reconnect, so this trip is important. Don't screw it up because of me."

She checked her watch; it was time to go. She turned to leave, thinking that she would wave to him from inside the airport. Instead, she stood her ground.

"Hey."

Her voice stopped him from heading back to the car.

"Yeah?"

"You should… You should call me. While I'm in Florida."

"Yeah?" A grin slowly spread across his face. "For sure."

"And when I get back too."

"Definitely."

"Cool," she said. Her casual words belied the butter-flies fluttering in her gut. "Merry Christmas."

"You too," he said, swinging her keys around.

They each waited for the other to walk away, and as Jamie began to haul her suitcase toward the entrance, a rush of emotion came over her. She marched back to Nick.

"What's the matter?" he asked, puzzled.

She stood on the tips of her toes and threw her arms around his neck. Each fresh scar on her skin stretched uncomfortably, but she forgot all about it as his hands slid around the small of her back. As she reached up to kiss him, she twirled that damn strand of hair around her fingers and brushed it out of his face.

"What was that for?" he asked when they parted.

"Just something I wanted to do for a long time," she said, adding, "Are you sure you'll be okay?"

"Jamie," he mock-groaned. He traced his thumb along her jawbone until he could tuck her hair behind her ear. "I'll be fine."

Ready to leave for real this time, she collected her suitcase and headed for the doors. She was glowing and bubbling with mixed emotions about the week ahead. Entering the airport, she paused only for a moment to wave and say, "Call me."

THE END

THANK YOU FOR READING!

Being an indie author is hard work, so I thank you for finding and reading my book. If you enjoyed it, please leave a review or tell a friend. Or review a friend and tell me about them. I like judging people.

— *S.S.*

ABOUT THE AUTHOR

Retro horror author Stephanie Sparks writes stories reminiscent of classic 70s and 80s slasher and monster movies. She loves scream queens, final girls, and the masked maniacs who stalk them. Her books feature action, thrills, dark humour, and sarcasm. She prefers cats to people, and when she's not lost in a paperback from hell or listening to 1980s movie soundtracks, she's day-dreaming ideas for her next book or writing furiously.

See what she's working on at StephanieSparks.ca.

ALSO AVAILABLE

More retro horror novels by Stephanie Sparks:

Kill the Babysitter

Jane's first babysitting gig comes with a lot of rules, and after a hellish night, she breaks an important one: *Don't let the kids play with the Ouija board.* Now the mischievous spirit in the board wants to play a deadly new game: *Kill the Babysitter.* Jane must fight tooth and nail against a murderous horde of possessed children — and if she doesn't team up with her worst enemy, she may not survive the night.

Scream, Queen

1984... Beautiful, do-good student Becca has been nominated for the coveted role of queen of her town's Harvest Festival. But when she starts looking into its history, she discovers that each of the past queens died under mysterious circumstances — including her mom. There is something insidiously rotten about the festival, and if Becca can't escape her queenly duties, she will have to make the ultimate sacrifice.

See more at StephanieSparks.ca.

PREVIEW

KILL THE BABYSITTER

Available now

March 2019

J ane Freeman was washing paint brushes in the sink when the Beast attacked her in broad daylight. Six feet of puffy, ruddy skin and brown eyes that simmered with hatred, the Beast wanted her dead from day one.

Everyone has had that one bully that scared the living daylights of them, that forced you to fake a sick day or beg your parents to homeschool you. But by the time you reach adulthood, the memories of those horrid people mostly fade away — or send you to therapy or the bottle. In the moment, all you can do is try to survive.

The Beast stalked the halls of Morganville High looking for trouble. Looking for Jane. Tall, wide, and menacing, the Beast was built like a rugby player. In just the few months she had been attending Jane's school, the

Beast had made Jane's life a living hell. Jane had no idea what she had done to incur the much bigger, stronger girl's wrath, but sometimes it didn't matter who you were. Anyone could get caught in the grinding wheel of high school.

That wheel had ground Jane down enough for several lifetimes. Her parents had divorced, and she hadn't seen her dad in years; her mom worked long, late nights at the hospital in town. She was a C-student with a paper due every damn week. And she was seventeen without a car, forced to take the bus to school and her feet everywhere else.

All she could do was fantasize about her dream car, a hot blue Mustang with black leather seats. Then she would be free, driving across the U.S. to retrace the old Route 66. And then she could finally have some fun.

Until then, she had to endure the Beast, and up until that Tuesday afternoon, she had been doing very well at avoiding her. They only shared two classes a week: Miss Smithers' chill-as-fuck art hour.

Maybe things had been going too well in the class. Jane was getting Bs (Miss Smithers handed 'em out like candy if her students simply applied themselves) and arguing less with the popular kids about the music they played. (Emily Burke and Brad Polanski and their goons swarmed the big table by the stereo so they could control the music, and they played Drake's droning, monotonous bullshit every chance they got, and then they shat over Jane's suggestions to play Ozzy and Led Zeppelin.)

So that Tuesday morning, when it was Jane's turn to wash the brushes at the end of class, she mindlessly hummed one of the less annoying Drake songs. A heavy set of hands slammed against her back — the Beast's paws! Turning to see, Jane knocked her hip against the counter.

"Ow!" she yelped

The Beast's puffy, red face was too close. Her hot, post-lunch breath blew into Jane's face. *"Leave me alone,"* she growled, before shoving Jane again.

Jane fell against the sink. The other students screeched back in their chairs, ooh-ing excitedly as they gathered around. The phones they weren't supposed to have in class came out in droves, clutched in trembling hands as a hush fell over the room. Everyone understood this wasn't the time for wisecracks.

It was time for a fight.

Jane gripped the brushes, watching the Beast stomp away. Her hip throbbed and her back itched where the Beast slammed into her. Her ego raged red-hot.

Without a second to think, she threw the brushes at the Beast's back. The Beast spun around, teeth gritted.

Jane turned to flee. Her sneakered foot landed on one of the brushes, and she skidded, falling face first onto the popular kids' table. Emily leaned in with her camera as Jane almost crashed into her.

"Extreme close-up," cracked a cute brown-haired boy. Nate-something. His blue eyes shined as he flashed her a grin. He only registered in Jane's world because her friend Lily wouldn't stop gushing about him.

"What is going on in here?!" cried Miss Smithers as Jane picked herself up.

The Beast fled the room.

After the conflict simmered down, the principal and Miss Smithers sent Jane to the nurse's office. She laid on a cot in the dimly lit nurse's office, holding a bag of ice against her hip, jeans pulled down low. The nurse asked her a million questions that her mom would probably ask when she got home. Eventually the nurse had to slip out to deal with another student and Jane got to lay back and stare at the ceiling.

She wondered what they were doing to the Beast. The girl was probably being yelled at by Principal Hector. Then she would be suspended, maybe even expelled. The school had a "no tolerance" policy for bullying and fighting — but that was only if the *school* determined it was bullying.

Regardless, Jane couldn't help but smile, imagining being free of that horrible girl for the rest of the year.

After about an hour of lounging around, Jane had company. The nurse shuffled in with the cute boy from art class. Nate. He sat down on the opposite cot and smiled shyly, trying not to notice that Jane's jeans were pulled down, exposing her bony, bruised hip. She didn't feel very voluptuous, but the blush that crept up his face made her feel self-conscious.

As soon as the nurse was gone, she sat up and adjusted her clothes. "Hey," she said.

"Hey," he said right back.

"What're you in for?"

He grinned and rolled up his pant leg. "Sprained ankle."

It didn't look swollen or hurt in any way. It looked like a teenage boy's hairy, skinny ankle. "Uh, what?"

The nurse poked her head back into the room. Age had etched deep, angry lines into her dour face. "No talking."

Both students nodded and waited until she was gone.

Then Nate took a seat on her rolling stool and cruised closer to Jane. Keeping his voice low, he said, "I just wanted to see the girl who slayed the Beast."

Slayed? Jane had replayed the fight over and over as she sat in purgatory. All she had done was throw brushes at the girl. She didn't commit murder. "What're you talking about?"

"The Beast is gone," he said. "The principal keeps calling her to the office. Haven't you heard?"

Jane had not. The nurse's office was the only room in the building that didn't have a speaker for the PA system. All she heard was muffled announcements from the hallway.

But she didn't believe the Beast was gone. More like "escaped." The Beast was loose.

She swallowed, thoughts flying through her mind at a mile a minute. "I need a car," she muttered.

She had needed a car since the Beast first started intimidating her. Following her home from school on a few occasions. When she tried taking the bus, the Beast would be there too. But a car was the ultimate safe space. The Beast couldn't get her then.

"I could give you a ride…"

She looked up. A ride was currency, but it was also used to barter. Cash, grass, or ass — nobody rides for free. She gave him a side-eyed look, summoning her usual bravado. "Sorry. I don't take rides from strangers."

"Even if I have candy?" he said with that damned grin.

Jane couldn't help it. She grinned back, running a hand through her messy, black curls. *No wonder Lily likes this guy. He's kinda cute.* "What's your name?" she asked, as if she didn't know.

"Nate Crawford," he said. Then he did something weird — he reached out to shake her hand. She let him, but no one had ever done that before. His skin was warm and dry, and he held her just long enough to make her blush. When he let go, she almost floated off the cot. "I'm pretty new here. Just moved last month. And you're Jane Freeman."

"Yeah. How'd you know that?"

He shrugged. "I've seen you around."

"Oh," was all she could say. "Cool."

"About that ride? I can't take you very far. Also promised a friend I'd drive him to yoga. But if you don't trust me — *yet* — bring a friend. I'll get you outta here safe and sound. It could be fun."

Stroking her chin, she pretended to mull it over. "Yeah, okay. I could use some fun."

Want more?

Order your copy today:

Amazon
Barnes & Noble
Blackwell's
Booktopia
Kobo
Waterstones
And more…

CPSIA information can be obtained
at www.ICGtesting.com
Printed in the USA
LVHW051644270821
696161LV00006B/760